Guitar Styles
from Around the Globe

Middle East

Your passport to a new world of music

JEFF PERETZ

Alfred, the leader in educational publishing, and the National Guitar Workshop, one of America's finest guitar schools, have jo forces to bring you the best, most pro educational tools possible. We hope you will enjoy this book and encourage you to look for other fine products from Alfred and the National Guitar Workshop.

ISBN 0-7390-3599-1 (Book & CD)

This book was acquired, edited and produced
by Workshop Arts, Inc., the publishing arm of
the National Guitar Workshop.
Nathaniel Gunod, managing and acquisitions editor
Ante Gelo, music typesetter
Timothy Phelps, interior design
CD recorded at Monkey Boy Studios, New York, NY.

Cover guitar photograph courtesy of Daisy Rock Guitars.

Contents

The author wishes to thank his wife, Neta, and his children Maya and Zohar, for their patience and support.

0

Track 1

A compact disc is included with this book. This disc can make learning with the book easier and more enjoyable. The symbol shown at the left appears next to every example that is on the CD. Use the CD to help ensure that you're capturing the feel of the examples, interpreting the rhythms correctly, and so on. The track number below the symbol corresponds directly to the example you want to hear. Track 1 will help you tune your guitar to this CD.

Have fun!

About the Author

Jeff Peretz was born in Newark, NJ, and attended the Berklee College of Music before finishing his education in Jazz Performance at William Paterson University. The author of *Zen and the Art of Guitar* (National Guitar Workshop/Alfred Publishing #21907), Jeff performs regularly with the Arabic jazz group Abu Gara, which he founded in 1996. He is also the musical director for Yemenite/Israeli singer Bat-Sheva, and has performed all over the United States, the Middle East and Europe. While his main instrument is the guitar, Jeff regularly performs on the ud and dumbek as well, including performances on ud with the Grammy nominated Latin group Yerba Buena. His jazz/hip-hop group, Jeff Peretz Group, has shared the stage with The Fugees, Groove Collective and Brooklyn Funk Essentials. He is a faculty member at both the Third Street Music School Settlement and the New School University in NYC.

Pronunciation Guide/Glossary

Abu-Ata = ah-boo-Ah-tah
AfsharI = ahf-shah-REE
Agam = ah-GAHM
Andalusi = au-dah-LOO-see
Artik = ahr-tik
ayali = ah-YAH-lee
Bakiye = bah-KAHee
Bashraf = BAHSH-rahf
Bayati = BAH-YAHT-tee
bazooki = bah-ZOO-kee
Belodi = Beh-loh-dee
Berber = Behr-ber
Buyuk = Buh-YUHK
Chiftatelli = Chif-tah-TEL-lee
Cins = sins
Daf = dahf
Darbukah = dahr-BOO-hah
Dashti = DAHSH-tee
Dhagstah = DAHG-stah
Dhagstaha = DAHG-stah-ah
Dum = duhm
Dumbek = DUHM-bek
e =
Esfahan = es-fah-HAHN
Fallahy = fahl-LAH-hee
Fasilia = fah-SEE-lee-ah
Finalis = fin-NAH-lis
Gecki = GEH-kee
Gusheh = goo-SHEH
Gusheha = goo-SHEH-ah
Hijaz = he-JAHZ
Hawzi = how-ZEE
Homayun = ho-MAH-yun
Huda = Hoo-dah
Idi = ee-dee
Ikili = e-KEE-lee
Jins = jins
Karatum = Kahr-TUHM
Kashlam = Kash-LAHM
Kayble = KAI-bul
Kitab = ki-TAHB
Kucuk = koo-SUHK
Kurdy = KUHR-dee
Layali = lah-yah-LEE
Mahgrib = MAH-grib
Mahur = Mah-HUHR
Malfuf = mahl-FUHF
Malhun = mahl-HOON
Maqam = mah-KAHM
Maqamat = mah-hahm-AHT
Maqsum = mahk-SUHM
Mashrig = MAHSH-rig
Masmoodi = mahs-MOOD-ee
Mizan = mi-ZAHN
Mucennep = moo-sehn-EHP
Nahawand = nah-WHAHND
Nasb = NAH-sib
Nava = nah-VAH
Nay = nay
Nubah = noo-BAH
quanum = Kah-HUHM
Qiyan = kee-YAHN
Quynah = quee-NAH
Rabab = rah-BAB
Radif = RAH-deef
Rai = rai
Rast = rahst
Rastpanjgah = rahst-PAHN-jah
riqq = rik
Sa = sah
Sama-I = sah-MAH-ee
Samarqand = Sah-MAHR-kand
saz = sahz
Segah = say-GAH
setar = SEE-tahr
Seyir = sah-EER
Shaabi = shah-ah-BEE
Shur = shuhr
Sikah = SEE-kah
Sinad = see-NAHD
Tahmilah = tom-mee-LAH
tabu = TAHN-bur
Tanini = tahn-NEE-nee
Taqsim = tahk-SEEM
tar = tahr
Taslum = tahs-LOOM
Tchahargah = t-HAHR-gah
Tika = TI-kah
Tek = tehk
Tork = tork
Ud = ood
Wasn = WAH-zin

Chapter 1 INTRODUCTION

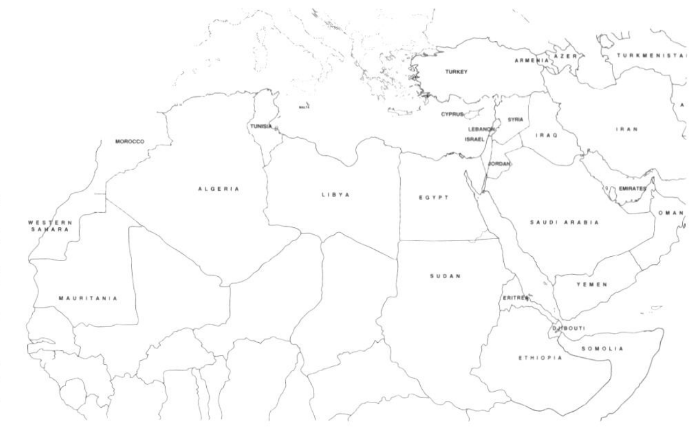

This book assumes that you are an intermediate guitarist with the ability to read guitar tablature and/or standard music notation. You should have a good grasp of basic music theory, including scales and chords. You should also have some experience using scales to improvise, although the style you prefer to play is not important. With this book, you'll be learning to create new sounds that will stretch your imagination, and the imaginations of your listeners.

About the Written Music in This Book

The written examples printed in this book are doorways into the performance of this music. The key that unlocks them, however, is the CD. The musics of the Middle East are aural traditions, and capturing them in writing is only partially possible. While the written music examples are not literal transcriptions of the performances on the CD, they will serve as maps to what you are hearing.

HISTORY

Music has been on the planet longer than humans have been recording them history. Archeologists have discovered musical instruments dating back almost 30,000 years; many believe that music may even predate human speech. Ancient Mesopotamia (modern day Iraq) is believed to be where it all started.

The Middle East is the birthplace of many things in this world, from civilization and religions to paper, our alphabet and recorded history (not to mention calendars and time keeping). It should come as no surprise that the Middle East is also a birthplace of improvised music. The music of the region that we call the Middle East is a tradition that has been cultivated for thousands of years. It is mentioned in the Bible and has been academically documented since the late 6th century. Many styles which are still played today date back as far as the Sassanid Dynasty (Persia, 224–651 A.D.), the Byzantine Empire (4th–5th century) and earlier. The concept of using a stringed instrument as a vehicle for melodic improvisation comes from these ancient styles.

To truly understand how the music of the region evolved, we must paint a picture of what life was like during pre-Islamic Arabia. The era that predated Mohammed and the birth of Islam was a time of tribal unions, trade routes and gypsies. From North Africa through the Eastern Mediterranean coast up to the Caspian and Aegean seas, and as far east as the Zagros mountains and the Iranian Highlands, life was defined by tribal association. Its story was told through the sung poetry known as *Layali*. The sung poetry was often accompanied by an *ud* (also spelled *oud*) or other string instruments that were light and portable and could be carried easily in a trade caravan.

There were three ways in which people lived in the early days of the Middle East. One either lived in an urban center such as Baghdad or Damascus, a rural region as a farmer or a shepherd, or you were a nomad (Bedouin/Gypsy) and traveled the land according to the seasons and trade. While each way of life had its own unique contribution to the musical development of the region, the concept of using a group of notes (scale) as a basis for free expression (solo) is a common theme in the ancient music of the Middle East.

The ud, along with the tanbar, saz, bazooki, tar and setar, all precursors to the guitar, are the key instruments in the development of melodic plucked string improvisation. The approach to playing these instruments is the genesis of the way we play the guitar today. In other words, this is where the pre-historic Hendrixs and Wes Montgomerys came from. It is the birthplace of the guitar solo.

GEOGRAPHY: FOUR REGIONS

The Middle East, or Near East as it is also known, is a vast region whose boundaries, depending on the subject matter, are often subject to different interpretations. As a matter of fact, the term "Middle East" is not inclusive enough for this discussion, since the musical styles being investigated here come from North Africa, the Arabian Peninsula, Persia and the eastern shores of the Mediterranean sea (which is usually what comes to mind when one thinks of the Middle East). Ethnomusicologists have taken to referring to the entire region as *the Dry World.*

The Dry World can be divided into four main zones:

1. *Mashrig* (where the sun rises)
   The Eastern Mediterranean—Persia, Israel, Syria, Iraq
2. *Mahgrib* (where the sun sets)
   North Africa Morocco, Algeria, Egypt, Sudan
3. The Arabic peninsula
   Yemen, Saudi Arabia
4. Asia Minor
   The former Ottoman areas—Turkey, Azerbaijan

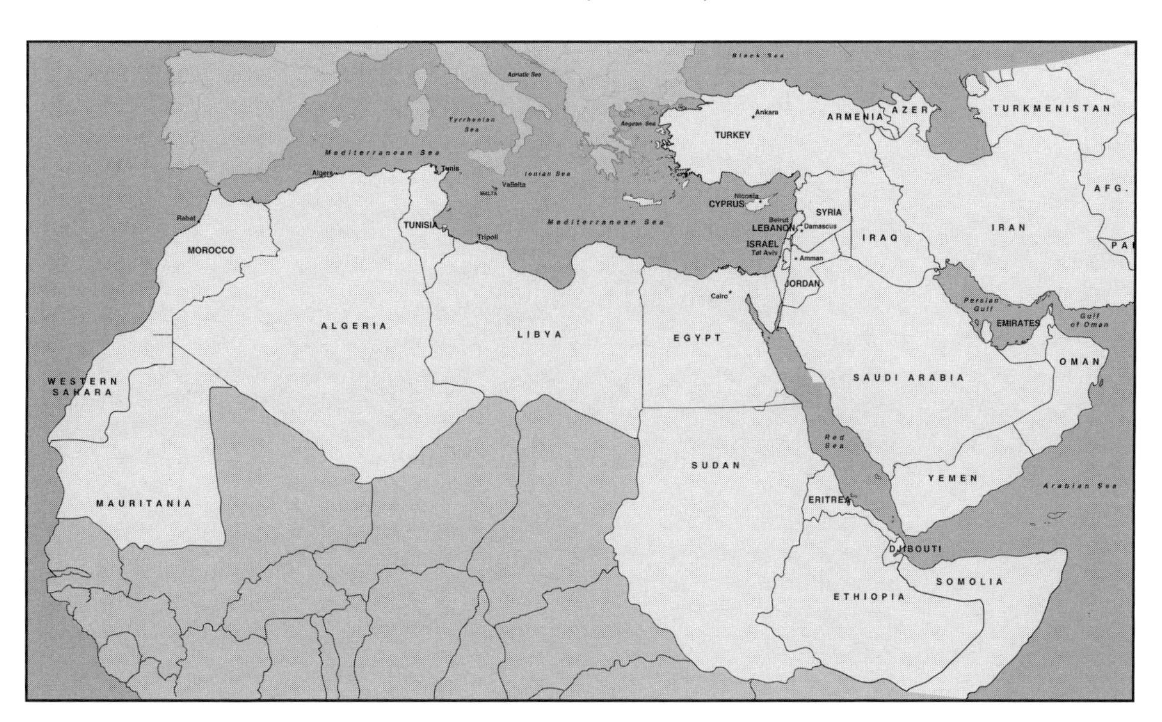

The music of each of the "big four" is distinguished by many different cultures, language and ethnic diversities as well as by geography. Early centers of Arab music include:

Baghdad
Cordoba
Mecca
Medina

From the 13th century on:

Aden	Beirut	Sanaa
Algiers	Cairo	Tetuan
Allepo	Damascus	Tripoli
Bahrain	Fez	Tunis

MUSICAL DIVERSITY OF THE FOUR REGIONS

Urban dwellers, rural farmers and Bedouin nomads coming from such distant places as Morocco, all the way east to Iran and from the Arabian Peninsula on up to Anatolia (Turkey) make up a huge population. Within this population, there exist many different ethnicities, cultures, religions and languages. The music of this population is like a tree with many branches. It is sometimes called "Arabic music," but as you will come to see, as well as being the music of the Arabs, it is also the music of the Persians, Turks, Berbers and Jews. In fact, the music of the Middle East is the music of all the groups who fill out the cultural landscape of the Dry World and they are all key contributors to the sounds of the region.

Middle-Eastern music can be divided into two main categories: 1) secular (folk) music; and 2) sacred (religious) music. The oldest recorded history of the music of the region tells of the *qiyan* (plural of *qaynah*), who were servant/slave/prostitutes whose duties also included singing. There were two distinct singing styles that were popular during the day of the qiyan. One is that of the Bedouin whose *Huda* (song of camel driver) and *Nasb* (song of remembrance) were mainly sung while traveling in large caravans. The other is the style of music associated with the non-nomadic.

The qiyan in the towns and cities were well known and celebrated for their virtuosic singing abilities. There were also two main styles amongst the non-nomadic population. One was the *sinad*, which were serious songs dealing with dignity and pride based on long, classic Arab poems. The other, *hajaz*, were folk tunes sung for entertainment and were usually accompanied by an ud, *dumbek* (drum) and sometimes *nay* (flute).

RELIGIOUS/CULTURAL INFLUENCE

Much of the music from the Middle East is intimately connected to the spread of Islam throughout the region. It is for that reason that the term "Arabic Music" is often used as a synonym for the music of the Middle East. For the most part directly linked to the spread of Islamic culture and trade, music was celebrated and highly valued during certain times and outlawed in others. The Koran never specifically forbids nor endorses music, singing or dancing and therefore has been subject to many different interpretations throughout history. The cultures of Morocco, Algeria, Tunisia, Sudan, Egypt, Palestine, Syria, Lebanon, Jordan, Saudi Arabia and Yemen are all intimately entwined with Islam.

Aside from Islamic influence, there are several other key religions and cultures in the region. These include the Berber people (indigenous people to the Mediterranean coast of North Africa), who speak an ancient language called *Kayble* and have a strong history of sung poetry that still thrives today. In Judaism, the prayer and folk melodies are grounded in the concept of *Maqam,* which is a set of notes with traditions that define relationships between them, habitual patterns, and their melodic development. Throughout history, the Jews have populated most of the countries of the Middle East, contributing greatly to the musical landscape. The effects of the Jewish *diaspora* (scattering), as well as the establishment of the state of Israel, have had profound effects on the music of the region.

Likewise, the effects of conquest by the Ottoman empire (1326–1923 A.D.) also had effects on music and art. The Ottomans were Sunni Muslims, not to be confused with the Shiaa Muslims of the Persain territories. They in effect took over the Byzantine Christian territory and combined Arabic musical influences with Byzantine modal *monophonic* (single-note, melody only) styles. In fact, the Byzantine empire and its orthodox Christian beliefs once controlled the entire Middle East and eventually shrank to include only Constantinople (Istanbul). The monophonic chanting style that was the hallmark of Christian Orthodox prayer has much to do with why Arabic music, for the most part, remained monophonic.

A book for guitar about Middle Eastern music is a tricky undertaking; it's like a book about squash for tennis players. The guitar is a relative (kind of like a nephew or niece) of the ud, saz, tar, tanbur, bazooki and setar, which are all featured prevalently in Middle Eastern music. The guitar, however, is not important in the modern music of the region and is absent from the traditional music of the Middle East. In fact, the traditional music of the Middle East predates the guitar's existence.

A serious problem arises when one tries to view the music of the Middle East through the eyes of a guitarist. As you will come to see, what makes the music of the Orient sound so different than the music of the West is that the music of the Middle East is not based on our 12-note, tempered system. The guitar, because its frets are based on a tempered system, is limited in what it can play. However, since the guitar has evolved as the modern Western version of its Middle Eastern ancestors, and since the approach and technique of the traditional string instruments of the region are very similar, it can be a worthy vessel to trek the sands of the Dry World.

The guitar belongs to the lute family as do all of the stringed instruments of the Middle East. In fact, the word lute is a Europeanization of the words "la ud." A lute is nothing more than an ud with frets, and is another very close relative of the guitar.

The word "tar" that is in gui*tar*, se*tar*, du*tar* and si*tar* means "drum" in most old world languages. All of the instruments in the lute family can be considered drums with necks and strings. It is believed that some type of guitar arrived in Spain from the Arabs around 1200. The earliest mention of the ud is around 300 A.D., although it is likely that some type of ud-like instrument has been around since days of antiquity (B.C.).

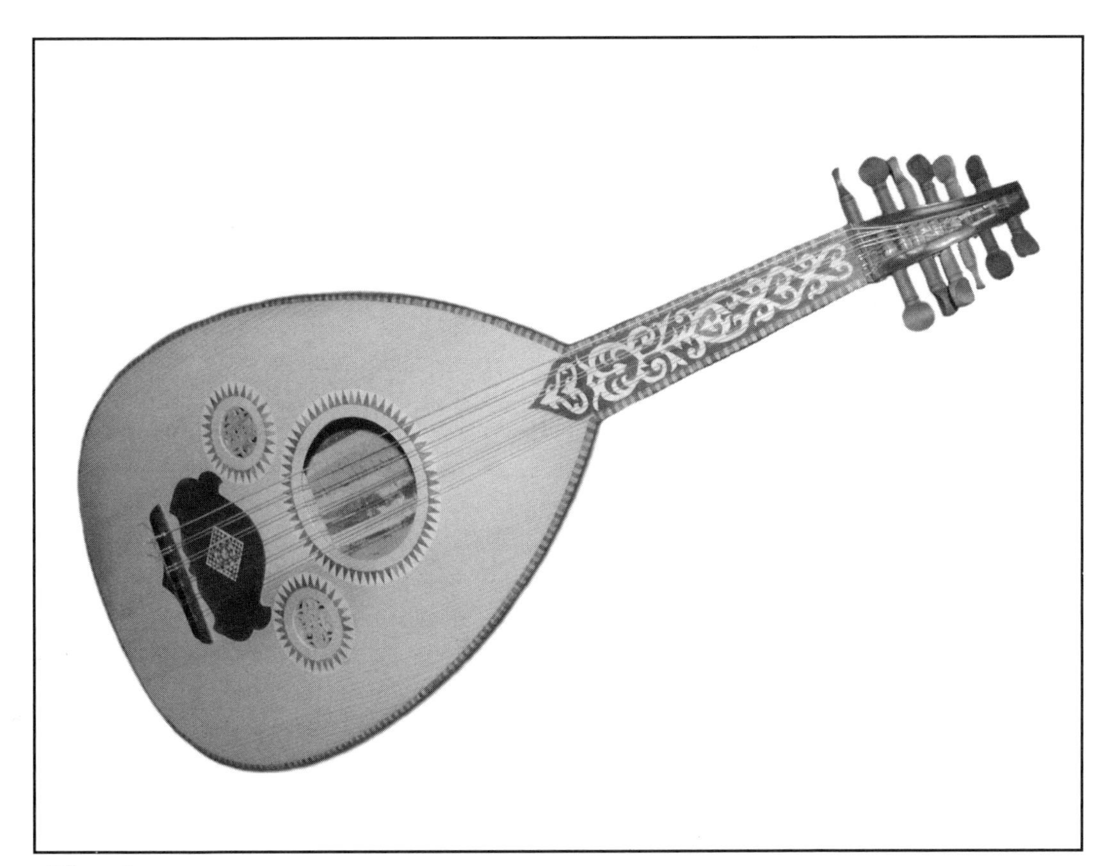

The ud.

Small clay figurines showing musicians playing ud-like instruments have been found near Samarqand (Uzbekistan) and date as far back as 800 B.C. There are also decorative seals and statuettes from Mesopotamia, circa 3,000 B.C., that depict long-necked lutes. The common thinking is that plucked stringed instruments are descendants of the *lyre* (an ancient instrument similar to a harp), which is also mentioned as far back as 3,000 B.C.

You will come to see that the ud is the most common guitar-like instrument in the music of the Middle East, and as such will be the focus of much of the study here. The saz and bazooki, as well as the ud, are important in the Turko-Ottoman regions and the setar is the main guitar relative in the music of the Persian region. However, the family tree of plucked stringed instruments has many branches. Almost every subculture in the region has its own version.

The Arab world doesn't, as of yet, have a "guitar hero." When the guitar is present, it is almost always used in a supporting manner that hardly calls for virtuosity. Many guitar players who are attracted to the sounds of the Middle East eventually pick up an ud, saz or bazooki. The techniques are so similar that most who take the plunge almost always find it extremely fulfilling.

The following diagram should give you an idea of the different shapes, sizes and string combinations that exist.

A Sampling of the Plucked String Family

A *course* is a set of strings, usually tuned in unison.

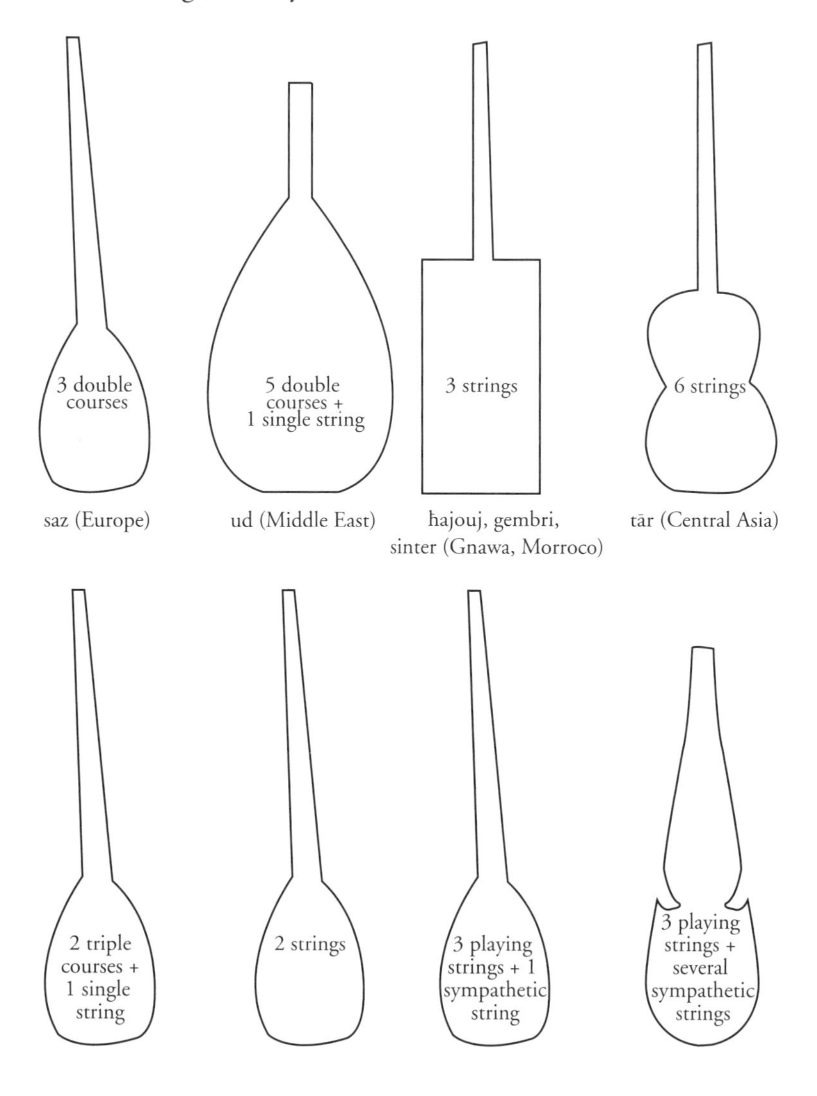

THE ARABIC TONE SYSTEMS

Given that "the Middle East" is an umbrella term for many different countries, cultures, religions and languages, and that the music was cultivated by trade routes, nomads and gypsies, there are many different ways in which the transfer of musical information takes place. In some cultures, the music is written down (Turkey, Iran), but not with our Western system. In most cases, the music is learned and transferred aurally—it is a tradition that is handed down from generation to generation, from father to son, and is taught through repetition and memorization.

Since Middle Eastern music uses a completely different tone system, using Western notation and guitar tablature to transcribe it can be a bit difficult. This is mostly because Middle Eastern music often uses notes other than the 12 tones that exist in our system.

In the West, we divide an octave into 12 equal pitches, but in the music of the Middle East an octave will be divided into 22, 24, 25 or sometimes even more different pitches. Herein lies the great difficulty of exploring the music of the region with a guitar. Our guitars are designed to express the 12 notes of the Western system and therefore will leave us needing to do some "tricks" to play other notes, and intervals smaller than a half step. To effectively transcribe Middle Eastern music for readers of Western notation, we must add some symbols that refer to notes that fall in-between our 12 notes, called *microtones*. As you will come to see, each region has its own distinct system of dividing on octave.

The common practice is to refer to the microtonal notes as *half flat* or *half sharp*.

𝄳 = half flat

𝄲 = half sharp

The biggest adjustment that a Western player must make to understand the non-Western music is in the ear. Hearing the non-Western notes can be difficult; at first they may seem to be "out of tune" or just plain wrong. Eventually, however, you will come to hear them as there own tones and be able to recognize their different emotional qualities. Consider how we recognize different colors. After all, colors, like notes, are a manifestation of *frequency*. Colors are frequencies of light waves and pitches are frequencies of sound waves. As a child, you begin to discern the different colors, starting with the primary colors. Eventually you are able to recognize the many different colors that exist between blue and red. The notes of the Western system are like the primary colors and with time you will be able to recognize the notes that fall between these Western, "primary color" notes.

Chapter 2 THE MAQAM PHENOMENA

As diverse and vast as the music of the Middle East is, one generalization that can be made is that it is melodic. There is one common thread that ties all of the music of the Dry World together: the *maqam phenomena*.

In its simplest definition, *maqamat* (plural of maqam) are melodic modes. But in reality the maqam phenomena encompasses much more than just a sequence of tones. It is an elusive, complex system for melodic improvisation that is subject to many different conditions. The music of the dry world, both sacred and secular, is characterized by these melodic modes and by melodic improvisation. It is an aurally transmitted art form which has been handed down from generation to generation, teacher to student, father to son, for thousands of years.

The folk music of the traveling gypsies and Bedouin nomads, Hebrew prayer melodies, Turkish Oriental Art music and the water wheel songs of old Nubia are all governed by the maqam phenomena. The playing of the traders and gypsies tend to pay less attention to strict intonation. They are more than likely found in nightclubs and not in the high courts or concert halls. Not only does the intonation differ, but the performance is more improvisation driven with less rules and structure.

HOW THE MAQAMAT ARE CREATED (TETRACHORDS)

Maqamat are based on three-, four- and five-note *tetrachords* (successions of four notes) known as *jins* that are extracted from the Arabic 24-note or Turkish 25-note systems. Each jin is a series of major, minor, medium or augmented 2nds. Much like triads are three-note extractions of Western scales and therefore building blocks of Western harmony, jins can be considered the building blocks of maqamat.

In the West, the main formula for creating a major scale is by using a formula of whole steps (W) and half steps (H): W–W–H–W–W–W–H. Maqamat are realized by sequencing two jins, one after the other.

There are seven main maqamat families (*fasila*). The jins not only give the families their names, but also their melodic colors, as they dictate the final *cadence* (ending) sequence. Each cadence sequence is based on the series of descending 2nds (minor, major, *medium* or augmented) leading to the tonic tone. A medium 2nd is a microtonal interval that is greater than a minor 2nd but less than a major 2nd. Each region has a different way of calculating the size, and even then, each individual player has a unique way of expressing microtones. Some are very strict (Persian classical) while others very loose (Turkish Gypsies or Bedouin).

There are seven primary maqam fasila. The following are the seven jins, their respective maqam and their cadence sequences.

M2	=	major 2nd
m2	=	minor 2nd
m	=	medium 2nd
a	=	augmented 2nd

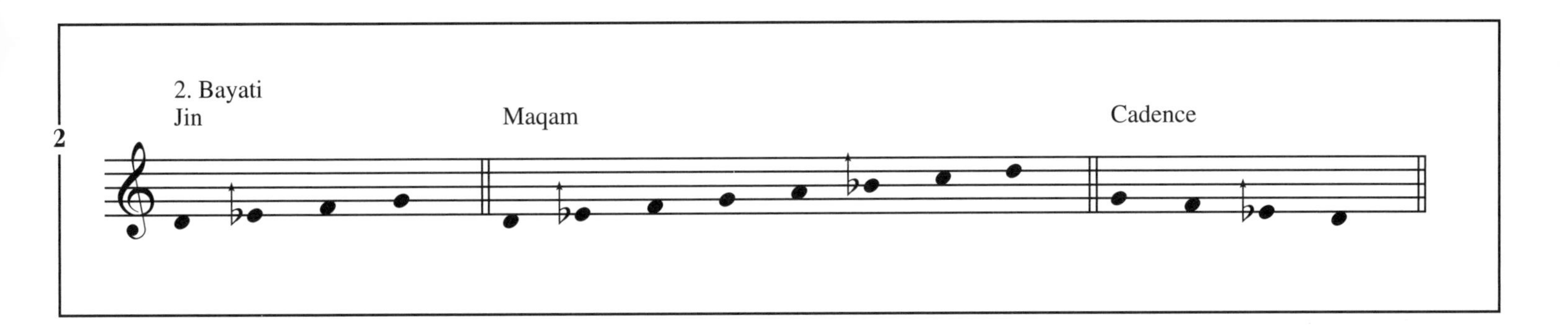

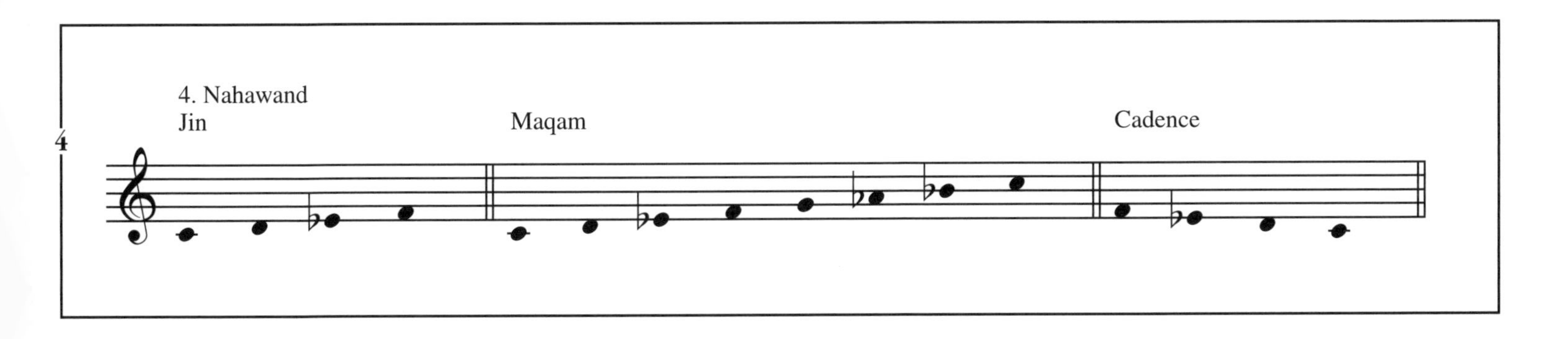

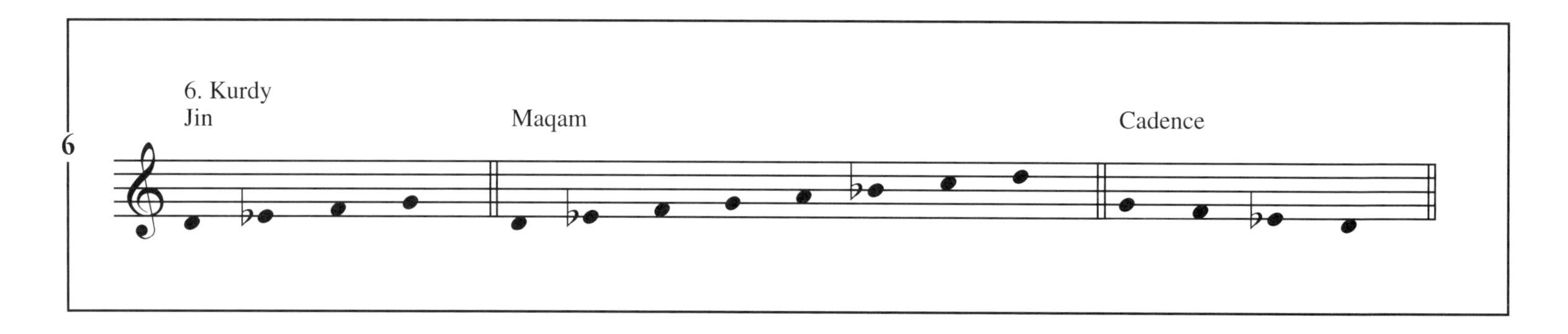

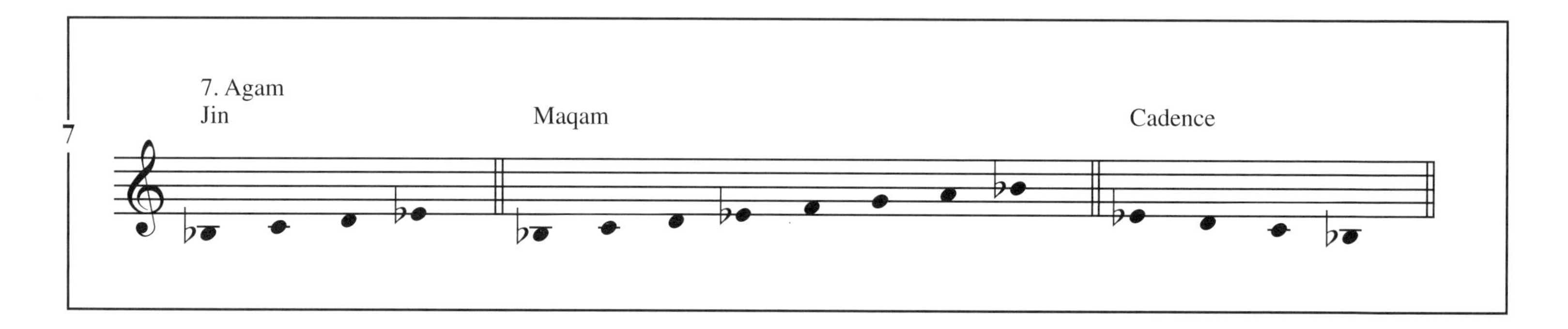

Modes don't necessarily repeat for each octave. For example, maqam bayati has a base tetrachord of bayati starting on D and then nahawand starting on G, which has a straight B♭ in the upper octave. It uses B𝄳 in the lower.

MAQAM PLAYABLE BY THE GUITAR

To properly investigate the depth of the maqamat phenomena, one must use an instrument capable of playing microtones. That being said, there are a handful of maqamat that are playable by fretted instruments. Many of them are also found in our Western systems. The following are maqam are all playable by fretted instruments and therefore will be the focus of our exploration here.

The tuning of the instrument is relative to the maqam being played. There is no real "standard tuning" for many of the Middle Eastern string instruments. For the most part, the instruments are tuned in 4ths, much like the guitar, with the lower strings tuned to key tones in the maqam for playing *drones* (a drone is a long, sustained tone over which improvisions are played). For our purposes, we will try to stick to as standard a tuning as possible, although rarely will we use traditional EADGBE. For the following examples, we will drop the 6th (low E) string to D for the drone and keep the rest in standard tuning.

Hijaz (Harmonic Minor Mode 5)

Notice the unfamiliar key signature. Unusual gestures such as this are needed to translate Middle Eastern music into Western notation.

The following diagram is the maqam Hijaz in D across the fretboard, with the 6th string tuned down to D.

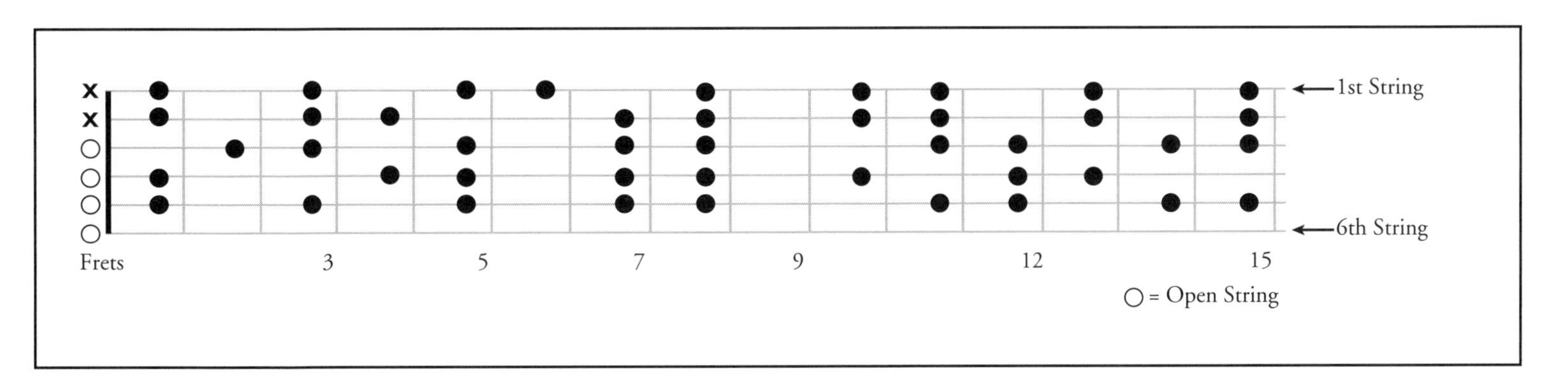

TAQSIM

The instrumental expression of a maqam is known as *taqsim*. Taqsim is a *rubato* (rhythmically free) improvised piece, usually played as an introduction to the more rhythmic expression of the maqamat. While the maqam is the basis of all Middle Eastern styles of music, the taqsim—the art of improvising using maqamat—is considered by many to be the highest, purist expression of Middle Eastern music. In theory, a taqsim performance is governed by structural guidelines (described below), but the success of a given performance depends on the improvisational strength of the performer.

The examples in this section are all part of the taqsim. In Western music, the intro is usually a small two- or four-measure phrase—a glimpse of something yet to come. In Middle Eastern taqsim, the intro is usually longer than the tune itself. The tune can be considered a simplified, rhythmically reduced expression of the intro.

There are several main rules to a taqsim performance. These include:

1. A **specific tone row** (maqam/makkam/dhagsta).

2. **Specific ways to begin.**
   A certain melodic figure which identifies the forthcoming maqam.

3. **Melodic unfolding/stereotyped motives.**
   Specific notes to land on, or destinations (read about target notes bottom of page 19), as well as signature phrases which reinforce the identify a certain maqam. The stereotyped motives are either commonly recognized melodies or sometimes just a favorite lick of a certain player or composer. A melody that attempts to capture the essence of a maqam is known as *seyir*. Besides the scale and its direction, the seyir might reveal typical melodic patterns, ranges to be exploited and notes to be emphasized, often leading to a modulation (change of key).

4. **Modulation.**
   As in Western music, modulation, or *gecki*, is a shift (either temporary or sometimes permanent) to another maqam or tonal center. Each maqam has its own *cins* or flavor. Most taqsim explore at least two different maqam as a point of comparison. For the most part, modulation is when different tetrachords that start on the same note are explored. Often, the modulation will have the same lower tetrachord but explore a different one in the upper half.

5. **Predetermined range and specific cadence (ending) patterns.**
   The range is determined by the lowest and highest tonal centers in the maqam. The specific cadence is the *taslum* or final descending pattern that concludes the presentation of the maqam.

   These concepts are illustrated in examples 13–17 and pages 20–21.

"Each improvisation by a master musician shows his knowledge and understanding of the maquam and its repertoire, his mood at the moment of creation, his personality, his virtuosity, and his musical (creativity) intelligence."

–Munir Bashir (great Iraqi udist)

Every taqsim performance of a maqam is an exploration of space (the relationships of notes) and time (the rhythm). In taqsim performance, there is no restriction of time or meter and no regular recurring measured phrases. The approach is similar to the Western concept of rubato. However, rubato is usually thought of as "out of time," whereas here that definition would need to be expanded to include playing in and out of many different "time signatures" or rhythmic groupings, as well as with none at all.

Likewise, there is never a fixed, predetermined form. Depending on the mood of the performer, a taqsim performance can last two hours or two minutes. What determines the length of the performance is how long it takes for the performer to reach all of the focus tones and then cadence. In this regard, the performance of a maqam is much like the telling of a story, complete with all of the different techniques used to tell a story effectively. Dramatic pauses, talking fast, slow, loud or soft all help define the emotional quality of the telling of a story. The same holds true for the melodic unfolding of the maqam. By the same token, sometimes short and sweet is the most effective way to get your point across, and sometimes a deep exploration of each tiny point is best.

It is safe to say, then, that taqsim—or the art of performing maqamat—is in essence melodic storytelling. Since no two people speak exactly the same way, no two maqamat performances will ever be the same. People of certain regions have dialects in common. Phrases, colloquialisms, patterns are often shared and come in and out of style, as do different melodic phrases. This is much the same as the blues licks that were played by Jimi Hendrix, Eric Clapton and Duane Allman. They are in the common language of blues expression for guitar.

Another key ingredient to telling an effective story is structure. Like a good story, taqsim have a beginning, middle and an end. Rising action, climax, falling action and building and relieving tension all play a huge part in determining the structure of a given performance/recitation. The concept of rising action, climax and falling action as a structural shape for a story or a taqsim are demonstrated quite literally in recognizing the important tones of a maqam. There is a common understanding about which of the notes in a maqam are "targets" and which are traveling routes. There are those notes which have a sort of "home base" quality and those which feel like they are leading to another note.

The notes which form the different tonal centers are characterized by their intervallic relationships to one another. Much like the concept of tonic (home), subdominant (pivot), and dominant (cadence) in Western harmony, some notes feel like home while others feel like roads to somewhere else. The intervals may vary, but there are always at least two main intervals.

The music and illustration on page 15 show the "what" of maqam hijaz. What makes a maqam become music and not just a series of pitches is the "how." There are several different *ornamentations* (melodic decorations, usually involving rapid flourishes) used to bring the maqam to life. The following examples are based on maqam hijaz in the open position of the guitar. Open position is the main position for maqam exploration because you can take full advantage of the open strings.

The following example is maqam hijaz in open position with open string ornamentations.

Picking ornamentations capture the essence of stringed instrument exploration of the maqam. The ud is traditionally played with a peacock quill, much the same way that we use a pick for the guitar. Often, what defines a certain player's style is his picking technique. The following example is maqam hijaz in open position with ornamented picking.

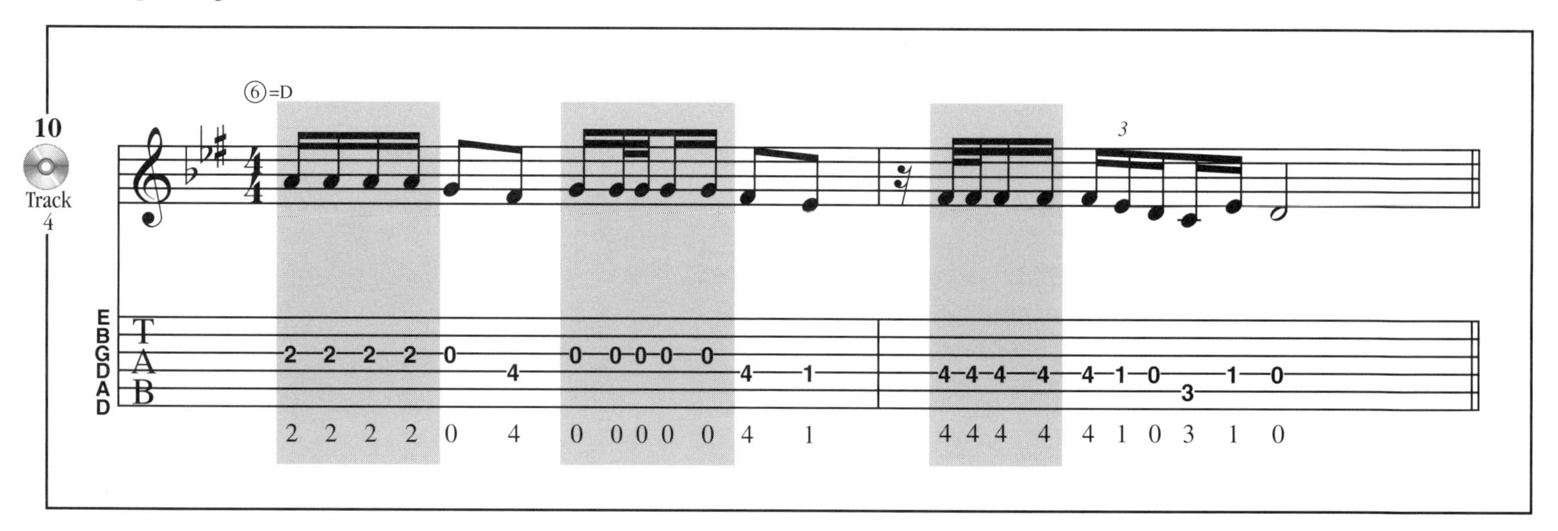

The following example is maqam hijaz in open position with ornamented picking as well as open string ornamentations.

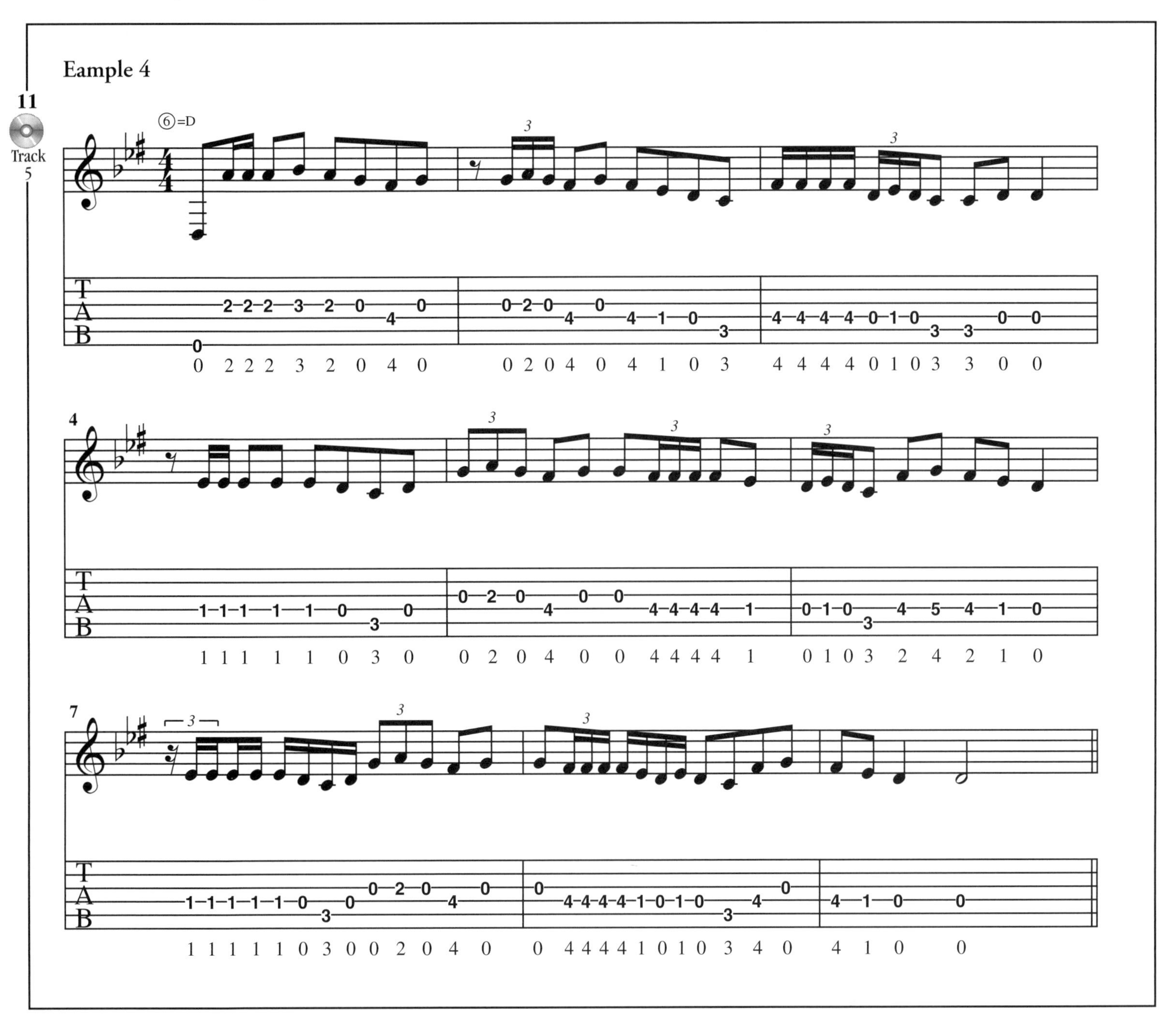

A *target note* is the destination of a melodic figure, and usually the focus section, known as a *phase*. Each target note can be considered its own "phase" of the taqsim. Generally speaking, the melodic development starts with the lower register and gradually makes its way up to the higher target notes.

The following example shows an extraction of the target notes in the maqam hijaz. Each of the tones is used as a melodic axis around which neighboring tones are played, emphasizing each tone as its own phase.

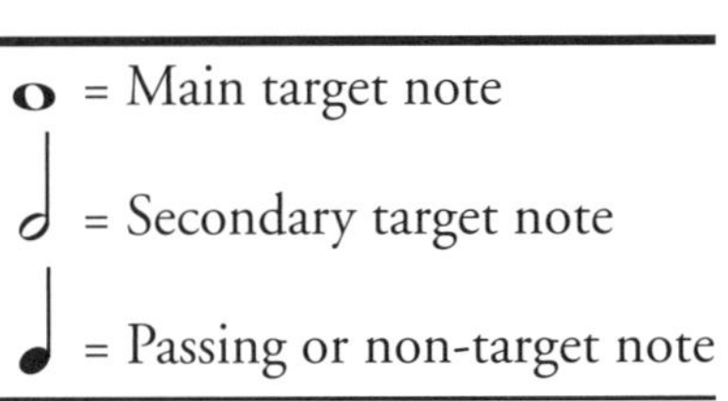

There are two main ways to explore a taqsim

1. Hover around a specific target note, as in example 13
2. Play with the interval relationships in a three-note group, or nucleus, of notes as in the hijaz examples 15 and 16 on page 21.

The following examples are designed to give you an idea of how a phase is created by encircling the target notes with neighboring notes, as in the first method described above.

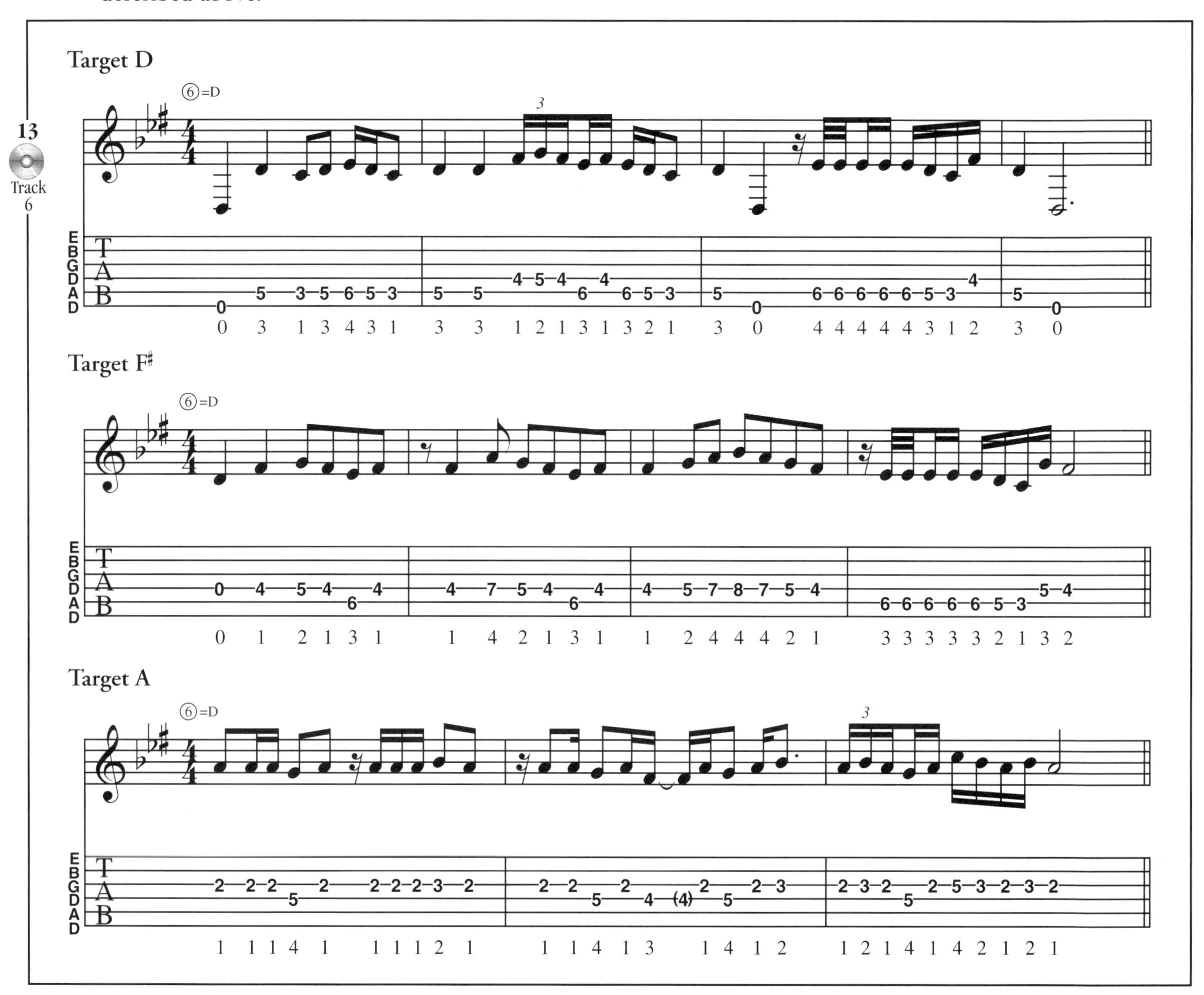

The second way in which the tones of the maqam are explored during a taqsim is to delve into the interval relationships of three note groups, or nuclei. It is widely believed that the emotional quality of each maqam comes from the sound of the different intervals that the target notes create.

If we take the target notes from the maqam hijaz (D, F♯, G and A) and view them in three-note groups, we would wind up with the following five ideas.

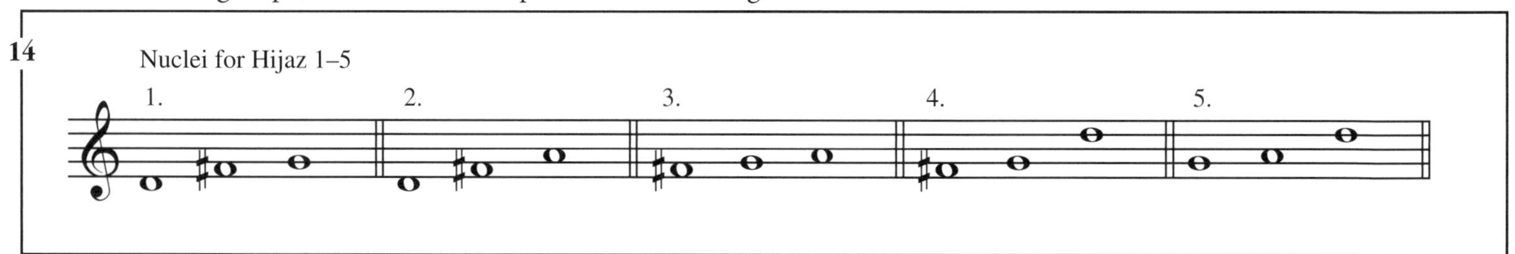

Example 15 explores Nucleas 1 from example 14.

Example 16 explores Nucleas 3 from example 14.

The final phrase which takes place after the climax of a taqsim is known as *taslum*. Taslum is the descending melodic phrase, known as the *finalis*, that leads back to the "home base," or tonic note.

While it's important to understand the theory and musical concepts behind the maqam phenomena and the taqsim performance, a large part of what separates taqsim from just running through the notes of a scale is the emotional quality of each maqam. Throughout the Middle East as well as India and the Far East, scales and modes and melodic groupings are usually seen in terms of their emotional color. For this reason there are certain restrictions—time of day, time of year, customary occasions and religious usages—that determine when and why a certain group of tones will be played.

We have a similar approach in the West, although we don't place much importance on it. We have the blues scale which sounds, well....bluesy, but "bluesy" is a relative term. Imagine if we called all of our scales by their emotional name. A major scale would be known as the "Happy Scale" and the minor scale as the "Sad" or "Longing Scale." The Dorian mode would be known as the "Funk Scale" and Phrygian the "Spanish Scale." To look at music in these terms would be to look at it like a Middle Eastern musician.

The following example is also based on the maqam hijaz. It begins with taqsim on hijaz and then goes into the tune itself, where the rhythm becomes fixed and the guitar is accompanied by the *riqq* (a small tambourine). Together the riqq and the guitar (filling in for the ud) explore several different tempos and rhythms, with sections that are pre-composed and sections that are improvised. Keep in mind that the rhythmic notation is approximate and relative (a whole note is a lot larger than a sixteenth note), but not exact. Do not keep a steady beat. Play as if you are speaking and telling a story. The music should sound spontaneous.

In time

Faster

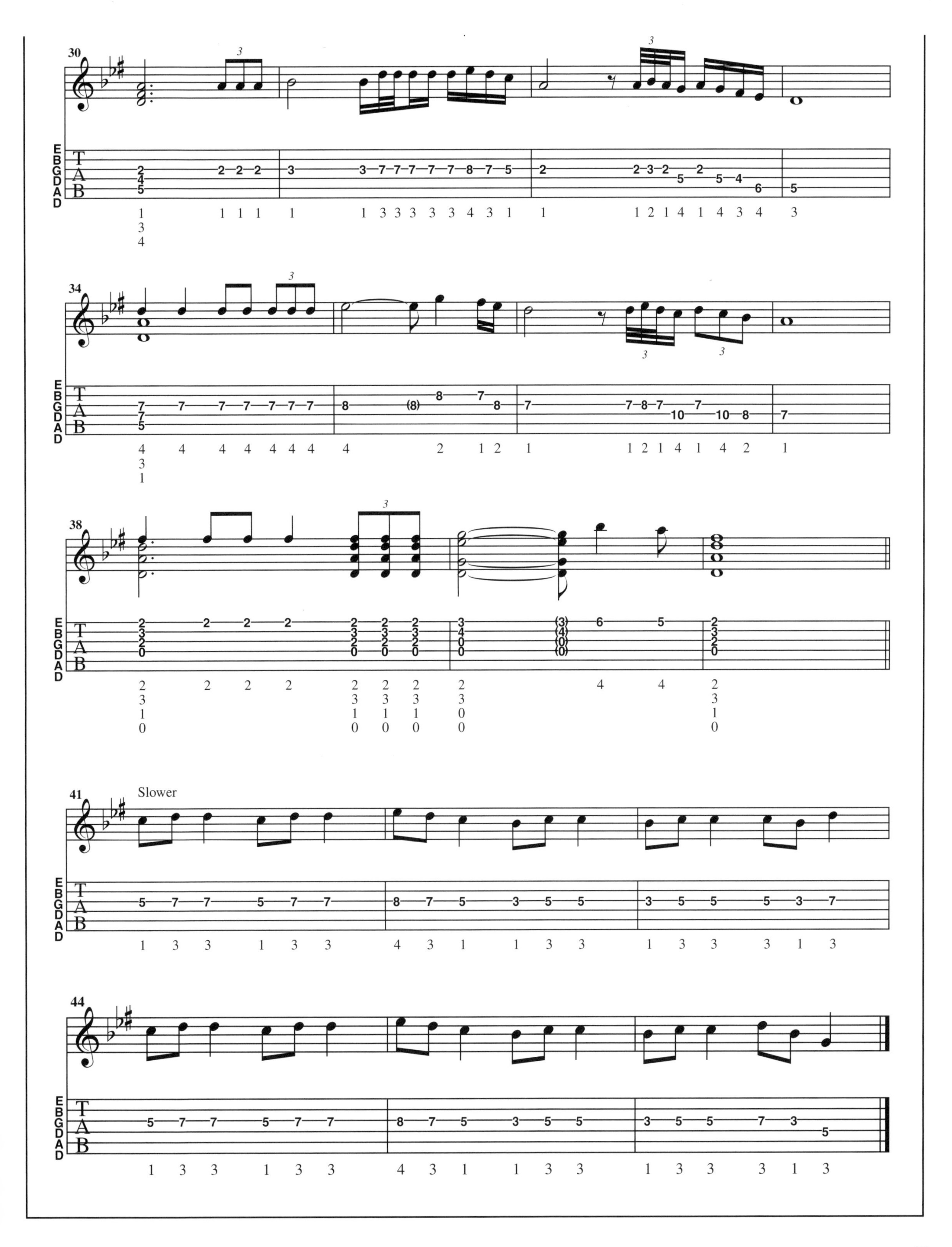
Slower

HARMONIC MAJOR/HARMONIC MINOR MODULATION

Munir Bashir, who many believe to be one of the greatest ud players ever, was born in al-Mawsil (Mosul) in Northern Iraq in 1930 and died in 1997. The city of al-Mawsil is known for producing great musicians as much as for its rich musical life. The musical lineage of the city pulls from a mix of cultural influences including Hellenistic, Byzantine, Arab, Turkish, Kurdish and Persian. To this day, uds can be found in most homes.

Munir Bashir was a student of Sharif Muhyidden Haydar at the Baghdad Academy of Music. Muhyidden himself was of Turkish and Arab descent and had studied with the Sufi masters in Turkey. For many, what separates Bashir from the pack as the most important of the modern udists was his deep grounding in the classical maqam repertoire coupled with the progressive, mystical approach that he inherited from his teacher.

The following example will explore the concept of modulation as it relates to taqsim and maqam improvisation. The opening section of the taqsim will be in maqam harmonic major (B–C♯–D♯–E–F♯–G♮–A♯–B) starting on B and then will modulate to Harmonic minor starting on E (E–F♯–G–A–B–C–D♯–E). This will be followed by the rhythmic expression of the maqam with riqq accompaniment.

This example is written in a key that would probably never be used in traditional Middle Eastern music, but it plays to the strengths of the guitar. The 5th string (A) is tuned up to B to give a drone tone.

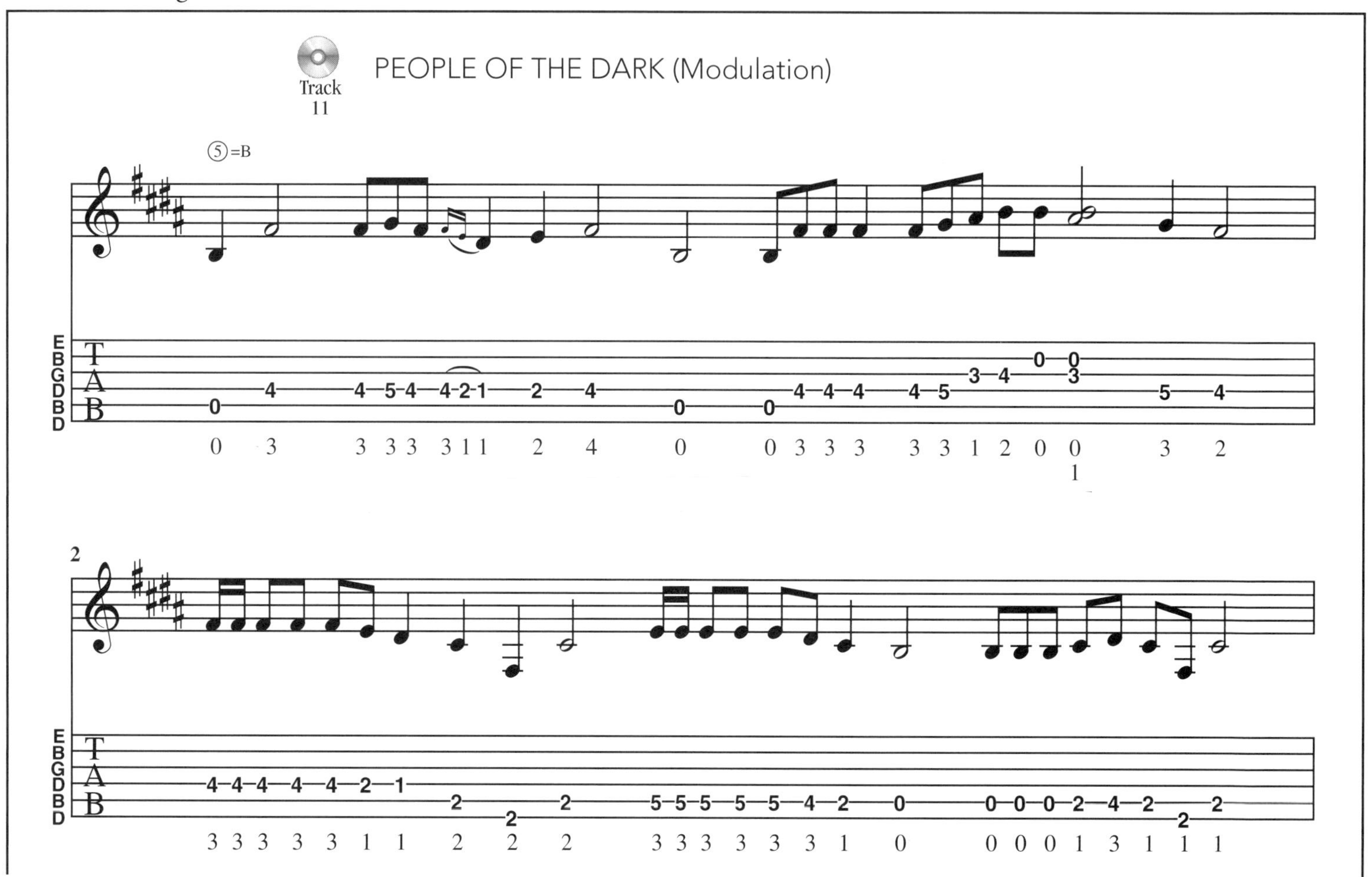

Taslum
In time
H P
H P

Easter

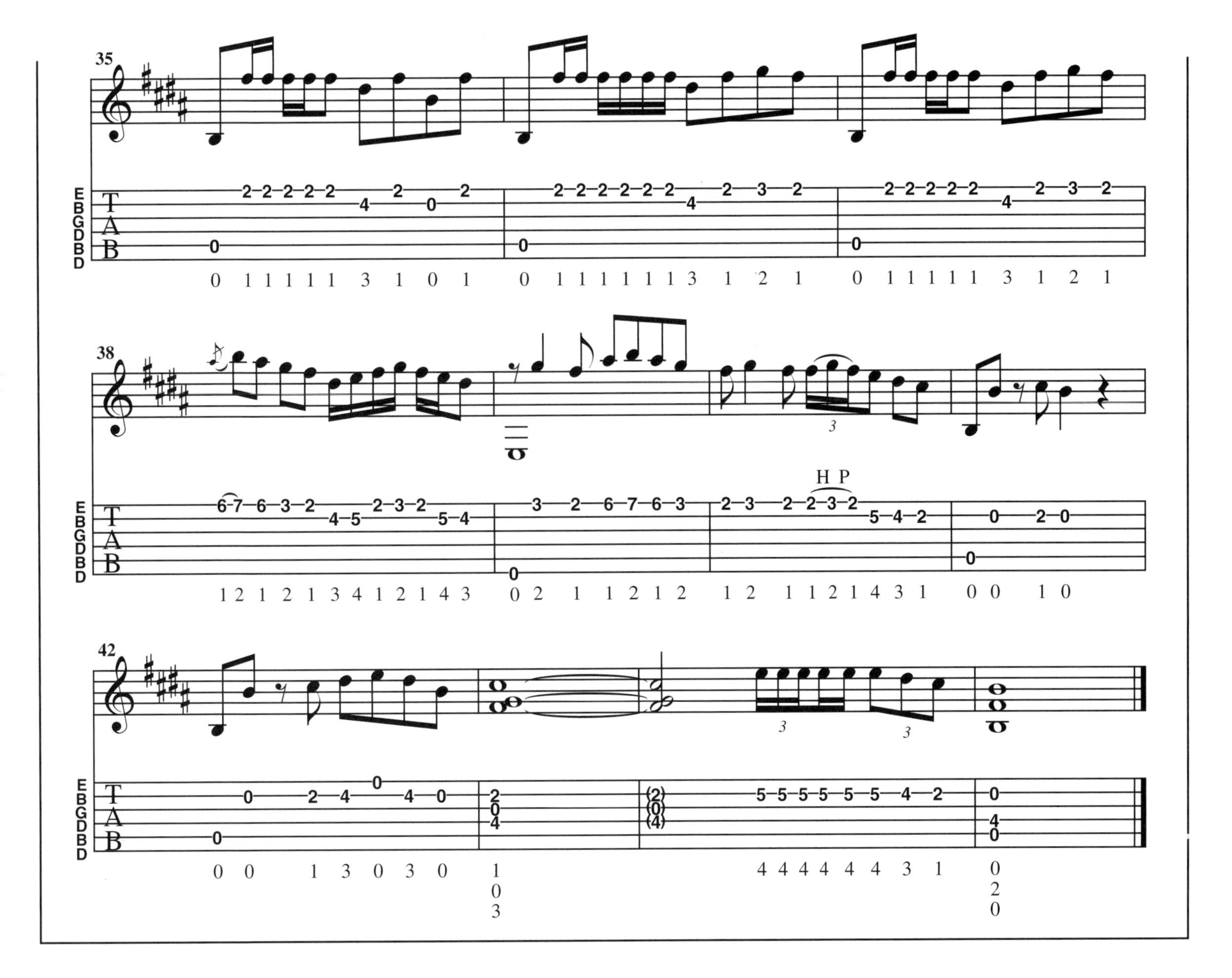

Ali Jihad Racy, the saz phenom from Lebanon, along with George Hadjineophytou and Huseyin Turkmenler from Turkey are three of the more accomplished saz players on the Turkish scene today. A saz is a long-neck lute of several sizes. Rooted in the classical song forms as well as the folk music styles of Turkey, their command of the makkamat and their improvisational prowess make them important figures in Middle Eastern music.

The example on page 30 is in the Turkish makkam *bayyati*. This example, unlike the others, is written in a makkam that does not line up with our Western 12 notes. There are some bending techniques that can be utilized to create the illusion of half flat. When a B♭ is used, it is played with the first finger and the string is pre-bent to find B♭, the tone between B♭ and B.

The saz is a three-stringed instrument that is usually tuned G–D–G. For this examplewe will tune the guitar's 5th string (A) to G and use only that string plus the 4th and 3rd strings in their normal tunings (D and G, respectively). While only the main melody notes are written in the example, all three strings are strummed for each one, thus creating the droning quality for which the saz in known.

This piece begins with a brief solo taksim and then it shifts into a rhythm. On the CD, there is a with a *darbukah* (drum) accompaniment.

Chapter 3 WASN RHYTHM

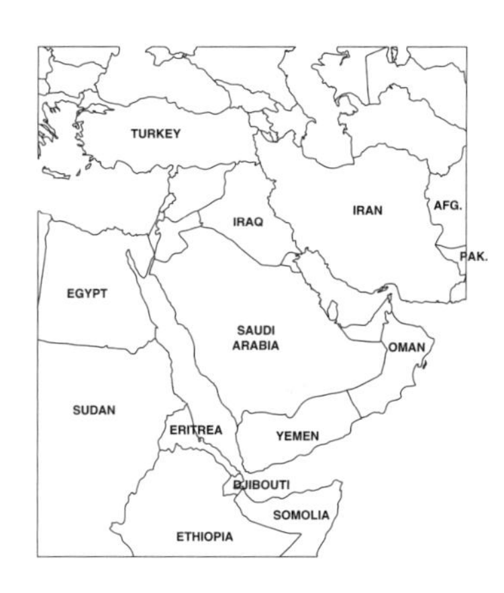

Just as maqamat are the Middle Eastern counterparts to our Western scales, *wasn* are Middle Eastern equivalents of our rhythms. The rhythmic approach to music in the Middle East is equally as complex and different from the Western approach as is the melodic system. Turkish folk songs are more often than not written in odd groupings of fives, sevens and nines. Persian classical music is through-composed and sometimes can go on for 40 or more beats before repeating itself. The *Samaai*, the most popular oriental art music form, is based on a cycle of 10 beats.

The main rhythmic instruments in Middle Eastern music are the *dumbek* (goblet drum with a fish skin head), also known as *darbukkah*, the riqq (tambourine) and the tar, (frame drum) also known as *daf*.

Many of the Middle Eastern styles are built on very intricate belly dance rhythms. The chart below will introduce you to some of the basic rhythms. Each box is the equivalent of one eighth note. In the Arabic tradition, spoken syllables are used to communicate rhythms. *Dum* is used for accented, low-pitched sounds, *Tek* is used for accented, resonant high-pitched sounds and *tika* (sixteenth notes) is for unaccented high-pitched sounds. Keeping a steady pulse, read the rhythms aloud. For those familiar with a drum set, Dum is the bass drum, Tek is the snare drum and tika is the high hat.

BASIC BELLY DANCE RHYTHMS

Maqsum	Dum	Tek	tika	Tek	Dum	tika	Tek	tika
Belodi	Dum	Dum	tika	Tek	Dum	tika	Tek	tika
Chiftatelli	Dum	tika	tika	Tek	Dum	Dum	Tek	tika
Masmoodi	Dum	tika	Dum	tika	tika	tika	Tek	tika
Sa idi	Dum	Dum	tika	Dum	Dum		Tek	

Following are some common two-beat and four-beat rhythms written in standard percussion notation. This will help you interpret the syllables.

Here is a common eight-beat rhythm in standard percussion notation.

There is an unwritten understanding between belly dancers and their accompanists regarding which rhythms and which tempos flow in what order. Usually, the dancer enters to a fast Maqsum to get the attention of the patron and then moves on to a slow, sensuous Belodi, which speeds up to a fast Sa idi. A technically proficient dancer will then dance to a more complicated Kashlam in rhythmic groups of 9. Finally, there is a recapping each of the rhythms before the climax in a fast Sa idi.

The following example would be like the second and third sections of a belly dance, starting with a slow Maqsum and then moving on to a fast Belodi.

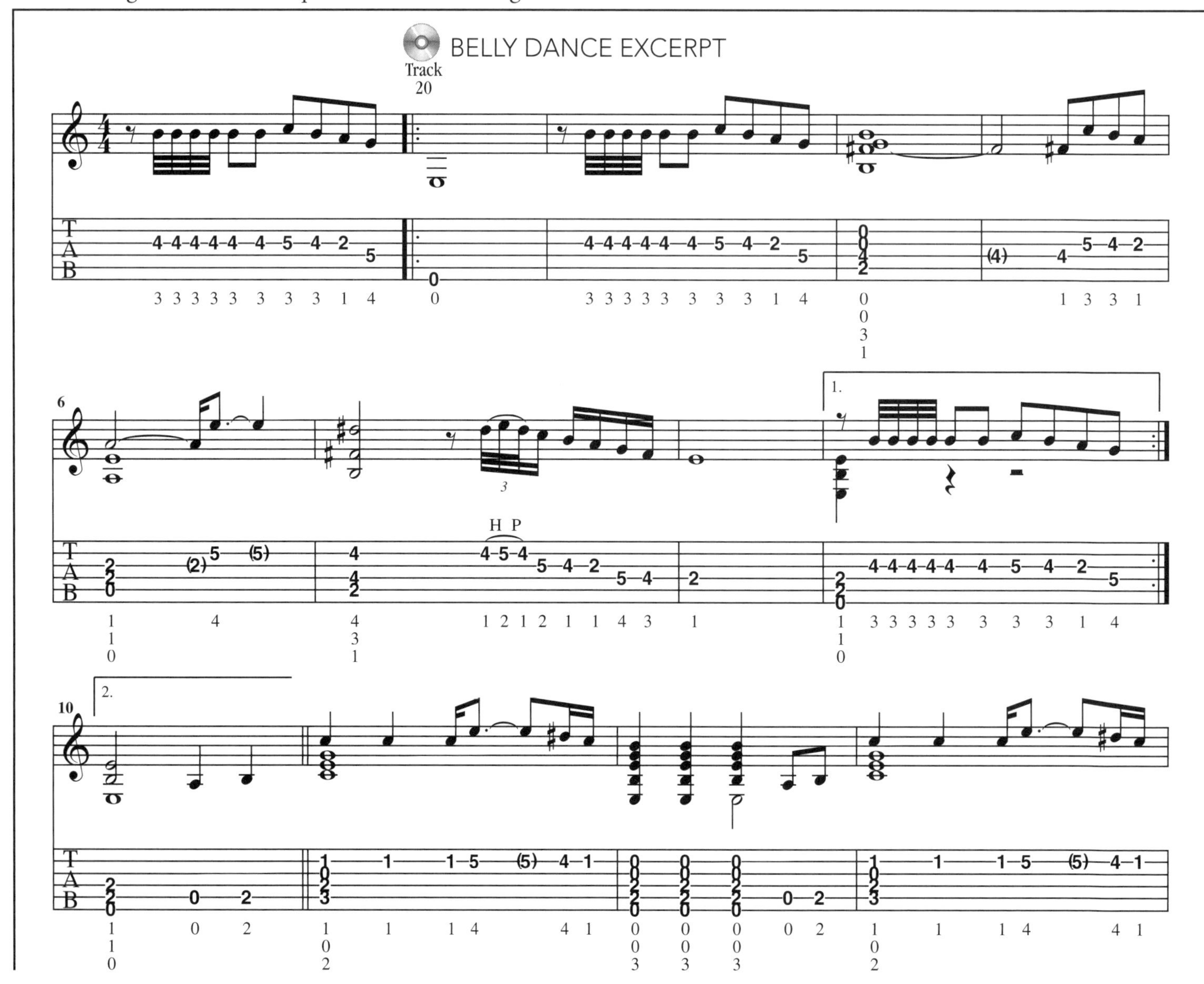

14
19
Faster
23
etc.
27
31

The following piece is based on the Maqsum rhythm. The maqsum is probably the most popular of the belly dance rhythms because it sounds like a Western funk beat, with the first snare hit on the "and" of "1." This rhythm is used by such popular artists as Natacha Atlas, Cheb Mami and Sheva.

This is in the style of the Shaabi music of the Hawzi Bedoiun of Western Morooco, which relies heavily upon the ud, which is very much a rhythmic instrument. A flute or vocal usually improvises on top of the rhythm, as well as hand claps accentuating a "2 against 3" feel. As you will hear on the CD, a performer will freely alternate between even sixteenths and eighth-sixteenth rhythms.

The following example is based on the Turkish *kashlama* rhythm, which is a cycle of nine beats used as an accompaniment to belly dancers as well as in folk tunes. The usual time signatures, $\frac{3}{4}+\frac{3}{8}$, tells us that there are nine eighth notes per measure, subdivided as follows: 1 & 2 & 3 & 123.

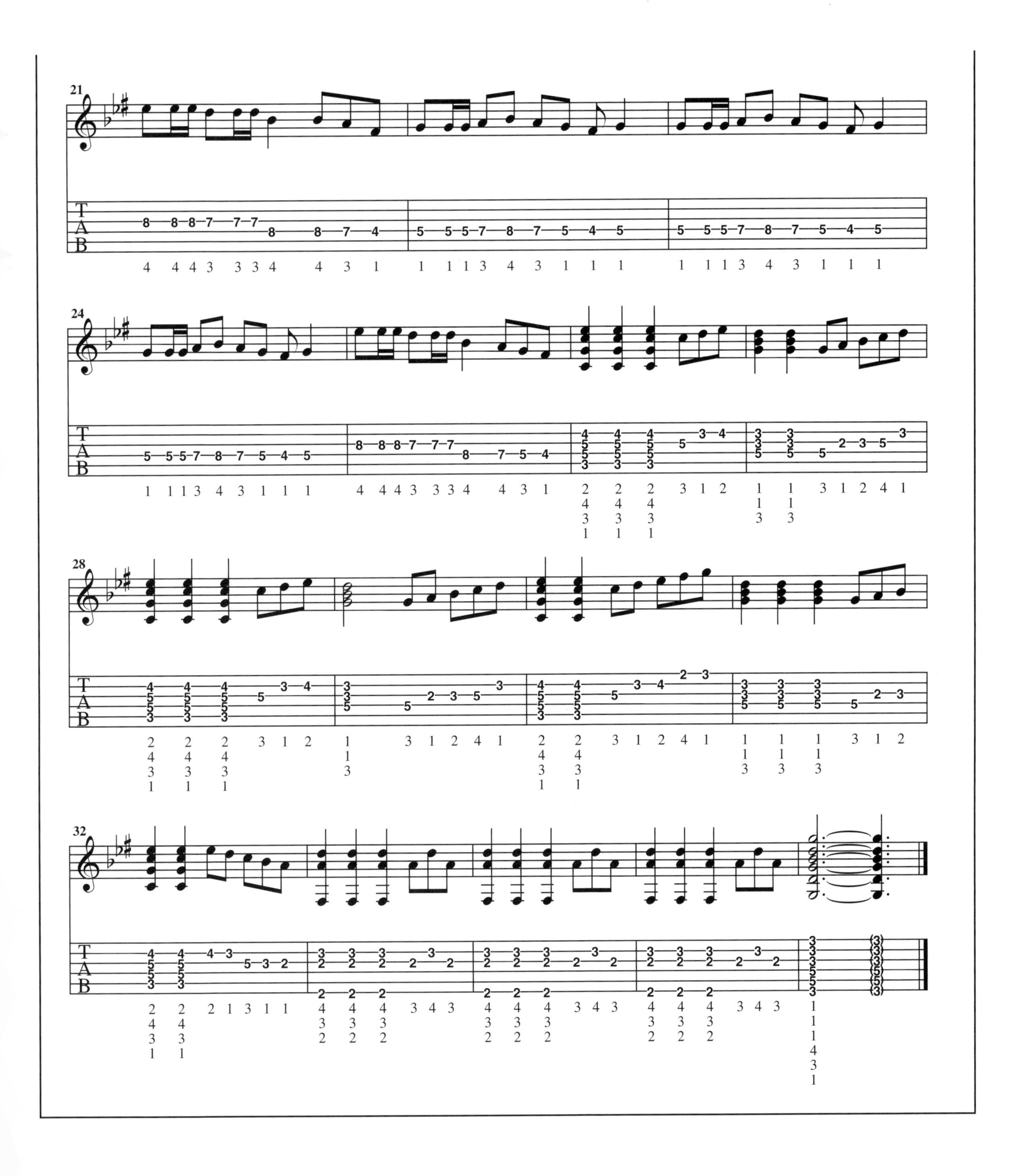

Chapter 4 MUSICAL FORMS AND STYLES

The many different song types and styles of song that come from the Middle East are vast. Almost every single tribe, village, city and country has its unique way to express itself with song. The easiest way to approach the immensity of it all is to focus on a few subcategories. These include sung poetry and classical "art music" styles.

SUNG POETRY

The *andalusi nubah* is a style which came from Baghdad to Qurtubah (Cordoba) and Grenada in the 9th century. It has five main sections of sung poetry, each proceeded by a short instrumental interlude. It is characterized by rhythmic intensity, and quickening tempos as rhythm patterns simplify. The Nubah opens with a taqsim which goes into an instrumental rhythmic section, during which the maqam is unfolded. This is followed by five poetry sections, each within a specific rhythmic cycle (*mizan*). For example, the rhythmic groupings might go from 6 to 8, or 8 to 4, or 4 to 3.

The instrumental ensemble that accompanies the poet/singer is made up of an ud, nay (flute), *rabab* (bowed lute/Arabic violin, held upright on the knee), and *quanun* (zither/hammered dulcimer), with the riqq and the dumbek filling the rhythmic accompaniment.

Another type of traditional sung poetry is the *Layali*, which means "Oh my night, on my eye." Layali is usually performed by one person accompanying themselves on the ud. Hamza El-Din is a modern day master of this style. Maqam phenomena rules apply.

Malhun, yet another type of sung poetry, is from Morocco and is played by male working class craftsmen. The stories are sung in the first person and deal with the trials and tribulations of being united or re-united with a lover. Aside from the two main characters (the desirer and the lover), the stories speak of a third party, who is usually someone against the romantic union who does anything they can, including abduction, to keep the lover from the desirer.

ORIENTAL ART STYLES

The history of Middle Eastern music is filled with colorful characters and great stories of how the music spread throughout the region. One such story of great significance is the story of Ziryab. Ziryab was a student of Ishaq al-Mawsili, who along with Ibrahim al-Mahdi were the two most renowned udist, singer, theorists of their time (the 9th century). The story goes that al-Mawsili was considered the greatest musician of his time and was a strict traditionalist. Al-Mahdi, himself already considered one of the greats after al-Mawsili, had been experimenting with a more free and open approach to music, which set him at odds with al-Mawsili. Two separate schools of thought were founded; the traditionalists led by the great al-Mawsili and the modernists by al-Mahdi. Ziryab, who was the top student of al-Mawsili, was also a proponent of the more open, less strict approach. Al-Mawsili, the strict traditionalist, considered this to be an unforgivable betrayal and banished the young Ziryab from his school, convincing him to leave Baghdad.

In 822, Ziryab brought this new style of Arab music to Cordoba in Andalusia (Spain). It was there that he created a school that is considered to be the foundation of the modern approach that is still followed today.

Tahmilah is an instrumental style which comes from Egypt and has much in common with jazz. Like a jazz performance, the Tahmilah begins with a unison recitation on a simple pre-composed melody (head) in $\frac{2}{4}$ time. This is followed by individual instrumental improvisations based on the maqam of the initial melody. The soloists often trade "licks" in a call-and-response manner. The performance ends as it began, with a unison recitation of the main melody.

The two most popular styles in oriental art music are *Bashraf* and *Sama-I.*

The Sama-I has four sections, the last of which is fast and asymmetric. It is played over a difficult rhythmic cycle in $\frac{10}{4}$.

Chapter 5 MODERN MIDDLE EASTERN STYLES

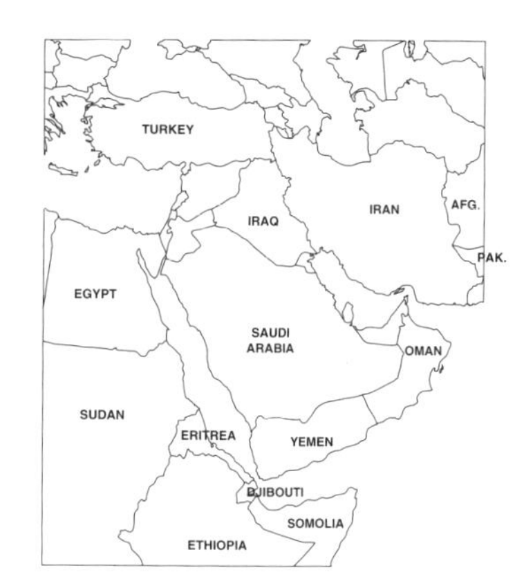

Since the guitar's arrival in North Africa in the 1930s, it hasn't really been used for solo Taqsim. It did eventually find its way to the Eastern Arab world, and it has been used for modernizing and interpreting local traditional and folk songs. There have been attempts at adding two frets to allow for playing non-Western maqam, but this never really caught on.

Ali Hassan Kuban's classic Nubian funk style of the 1970s helped create acceptance of Western sounds in the Middle East, much like Fela Kuti in Nigeria and Bob Marley in Jamaica. Ali Hassan Kuban's classic album, *Walk Like a Nubian*, was among the first to include guitars. In the subsequent 30 years, the pop music trends and production styles of America and Europe have been melded with the strong local folk roots to create what some refer to as "Arab pop." Again, painting the entire region with the same brush is not a great idea. There are many different styles coming from many different regions and countries.

RAI

One of the most popular styles of music in the world comes from Algeria. *Rai*, which literally translates into "an opinion" is the voice of the younger generations. It has been said that rai is to Western Algeria as reggae is to Jamaica. Khaled of Oran, considered "The king of rai," uses guitar on many of his recordings, some of which are produced by Western producers such as Don Was.

The following example is in the Rai style, and has the 6th string tuned down to D.

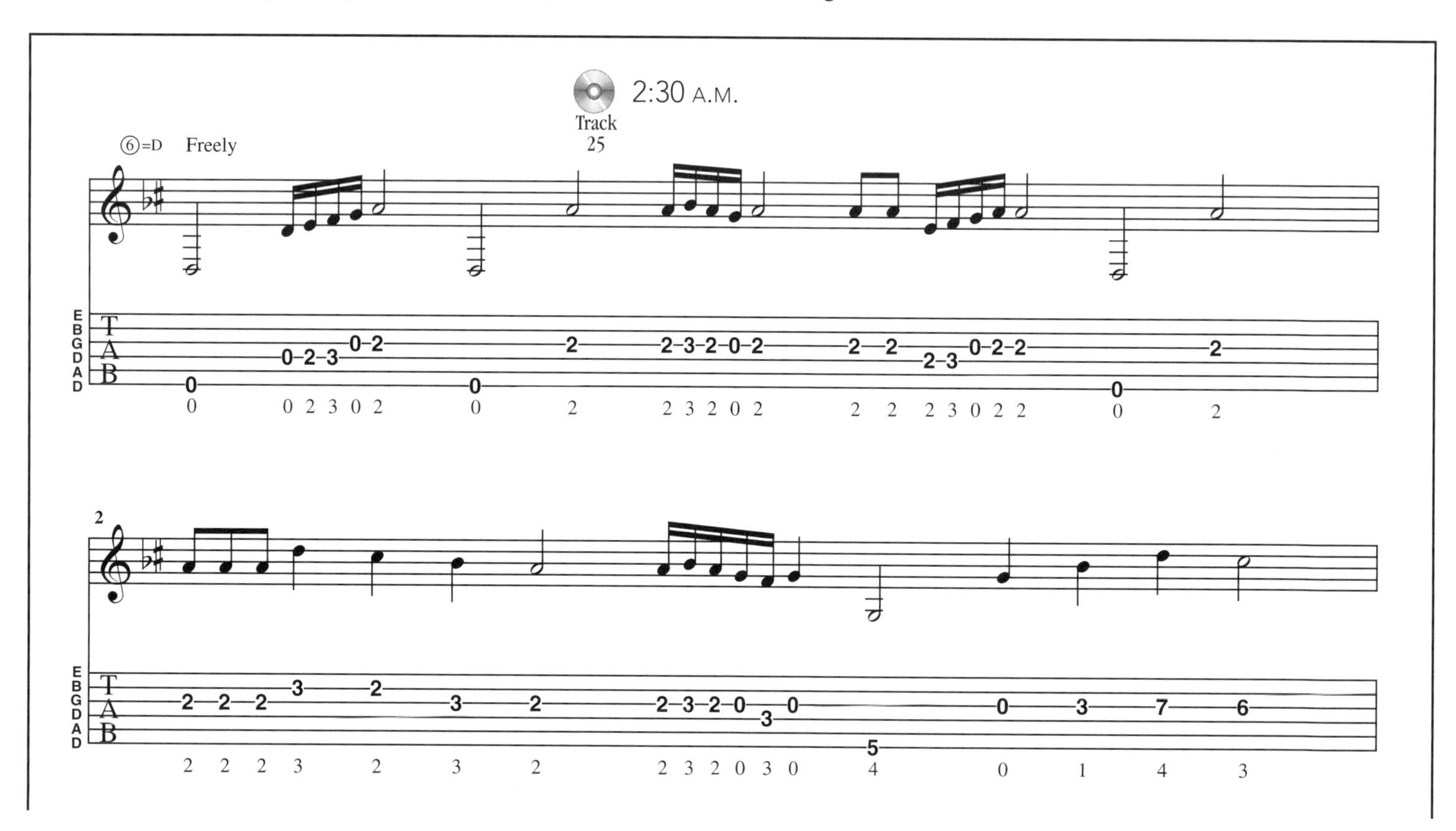

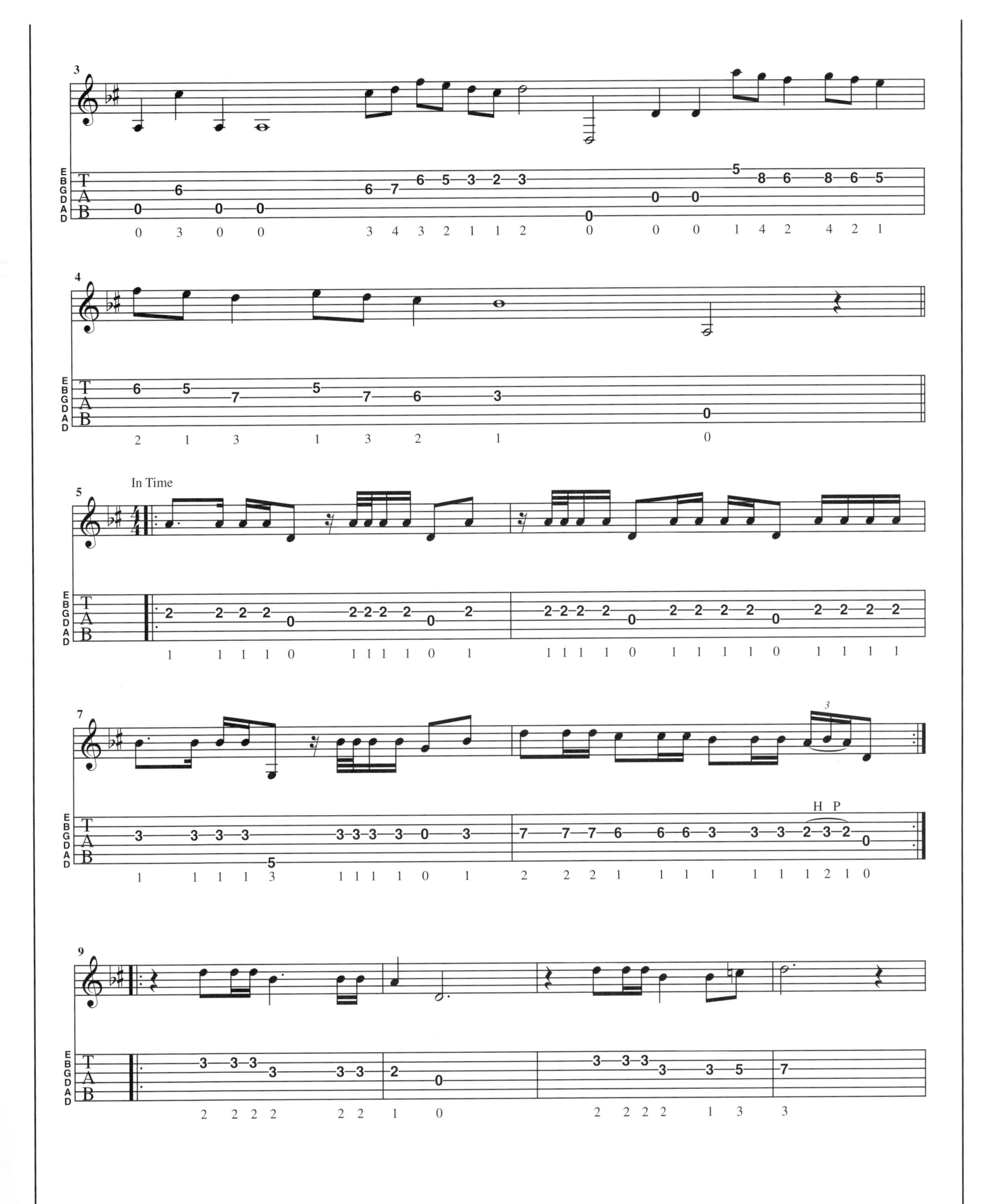
In Time
H P

13
16

20

25
Freely

OTHER STYLES AND ARTISTS

Other than rai, there is also another popular style of music which is played by the Berber population. The mandola virtuoso Abdelli plays mandola much like the guitar and has used acoustic and electric guitars on his records. Abdelli records in France as do many of the Algerian rai stars.

Here is a short list of other important contemporary artists of the region:

Fareed el Atrachi—Composer, ud player used guitar in his hit, "Habeena."

Fairuz Beirut—Second most popular singer. Used ud, electric bass and sometimes guitar.

Yair Dalal—From Israel, is known for both his guitar, violin and ud playing. Along with the Ziryab trio, which features Taiseer Elias on ud, Yair's group, the AL OL ensemble, are known as leading advocates for the presentation of Oriental art music as well as leading artists in the modernization of the style.

Amir Diab from Port Said, Egypt—Wrote "Nour el Ain," one of the biggest hits of the Arab world, which uses acoustic guitar strumming chords in a minor key. This music called "Mediterranean pop."

Ahmed Fat'hi—Lives in Egypt and is originally from Yemen. He is a singer and ud virtuoso.

Walid Toufic of Tripoli, Syria—Like many of the new "stars," he is a classically trained udist. His music includes flamenco-style guitar playing.

Other regional popular styles include Gulf pop (Nubia Kaliji, Arab peninsula), Malhun (pop music from Morocco), Uzbeki pop, Uighur pop, and Mizrahi.

The following example is in the folk style of old Nubia. It is in a maqam that is the equivalent of harmonic major. Much like the modernization of Yair Dalal's ALOL ensemble, there is a section in which the harmony shifts into the Western Dorian mode bar 25). The song begins with a solo taqsim and, on the CD, is eventually joined by percussion in the maqsum rhythm. In keeping with tradition, a modulation to maqam hijaz also occurs (bar 29).

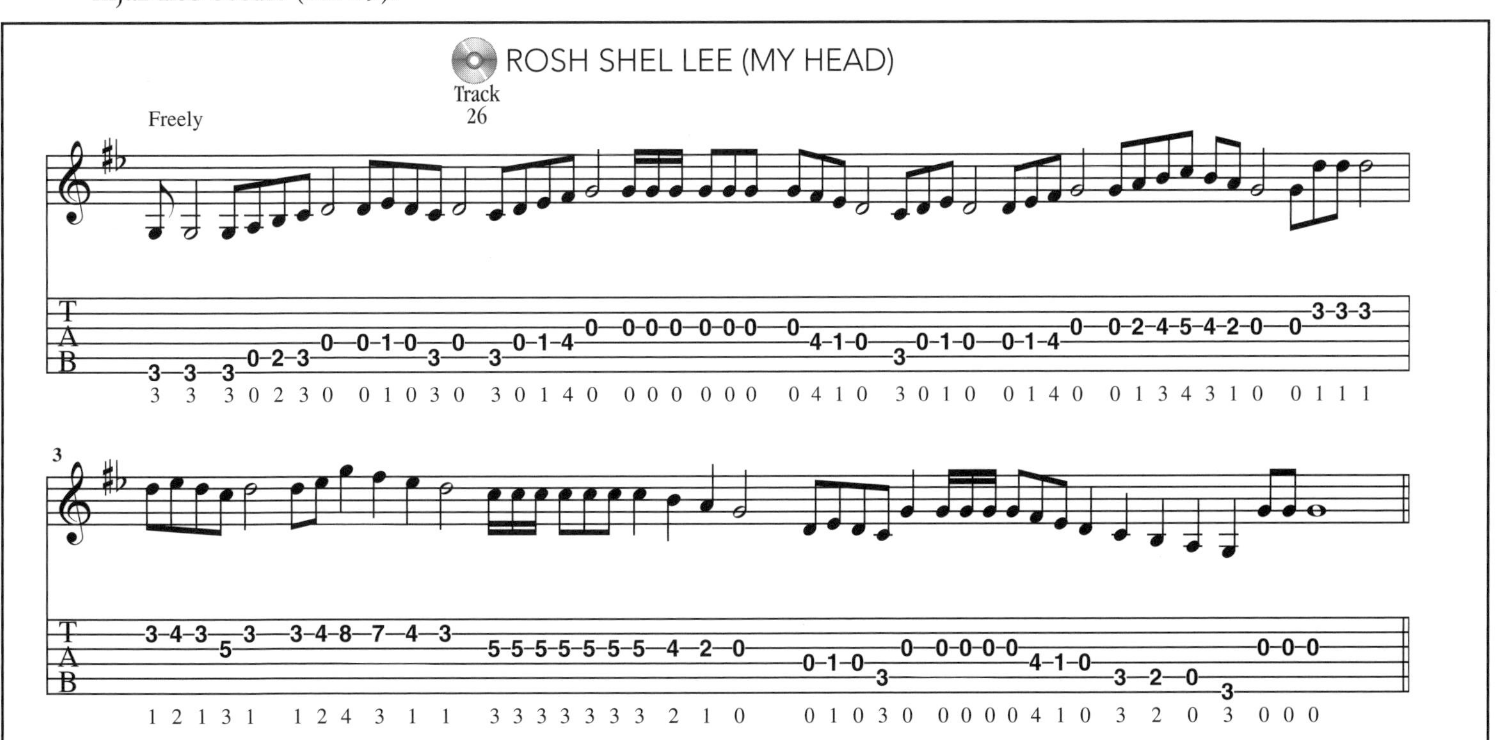

In Time
5
9
13
17
21
H
H P

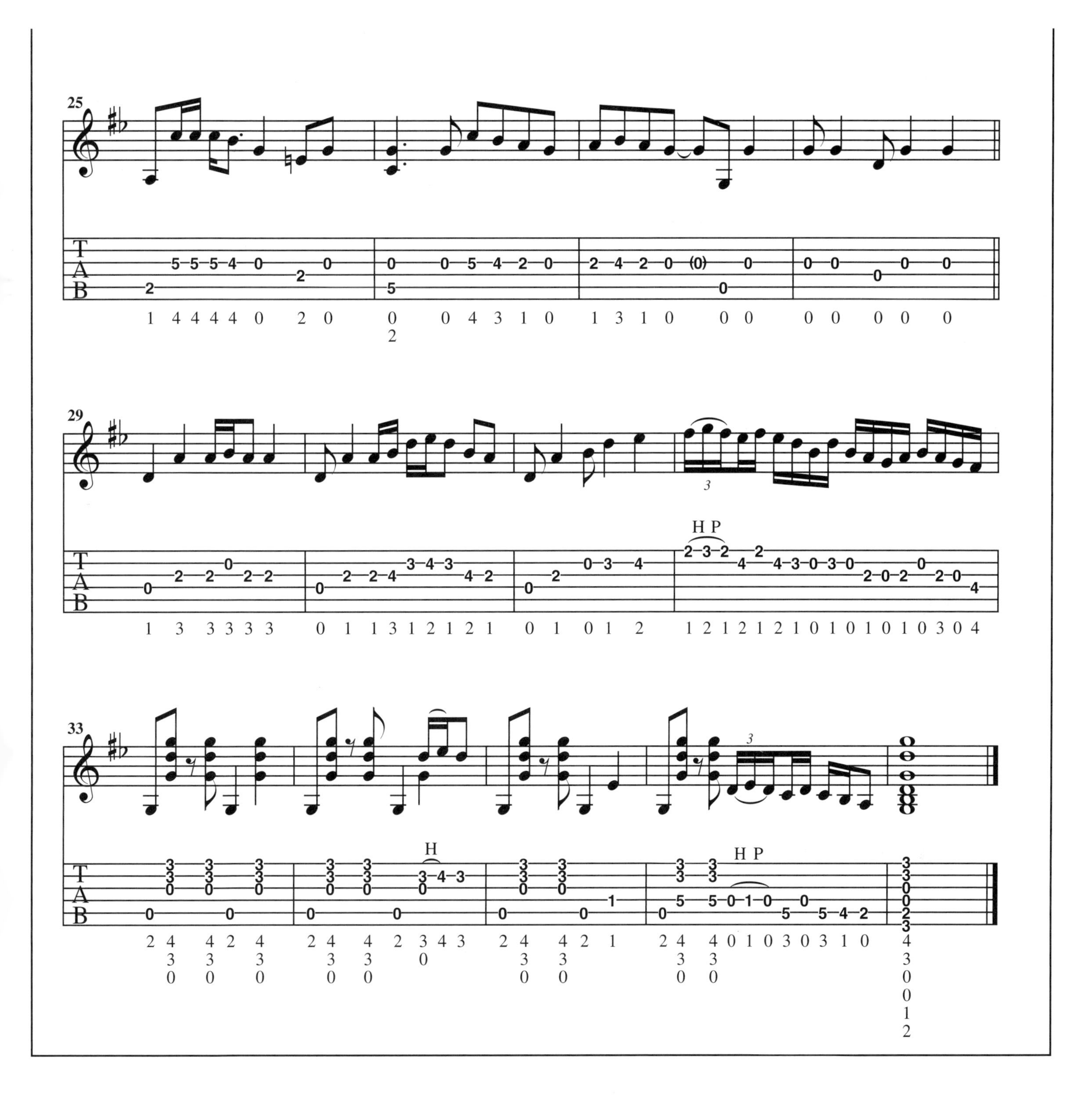

Congratulations! You have reached the end of this introduction to the music of the Middle East. As you can see, exploring this huge body of music could be a lifetime pursuit. But even if you never go beyond a little experimentation, those mind-opening experiences will forever influence your playing.

Have fun!

Appendix

MODERN MIDDLE EASTERN STYLES

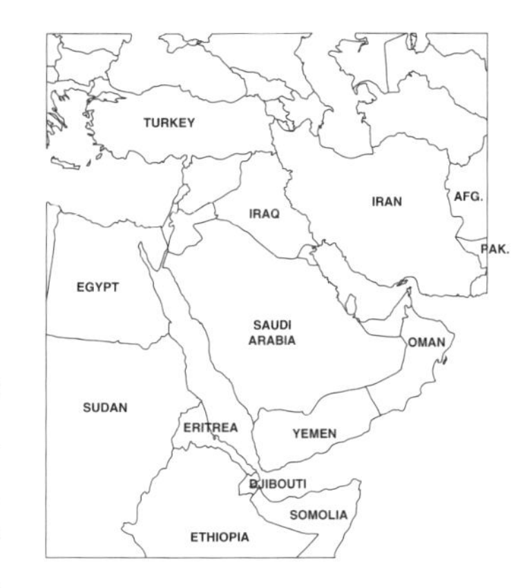

As if it's not difficult enough dividing an octave into at least twice as many parts, it's done differently depending on where one is in the Middle East. Historically speaking, there are two mathematical systems which have evolved into the two main systems in use today. One is the Greek system, based on the calculations of Safi ad-Din al-Urmawi in the 13th century, which is the basis for the Turkish and Persian systems today. The other is the Arabian system described by al-Farabi in the 10th century in his book *Kitab al-Musiqa* (*The Book of Music*). These calculations are not unlike the Pythagorean system that was crucial to the development of Western music, the main difference being that the ancient tone systems are all relative. There is still no fixed pitch as has ultimately developed in Western music (in the late 17th century), where the pitch A always equals 440 cycles per second.

The common and most effective way of explaining and comparing tonal systems is to use units of measure called *cents* (see Hermann von Helmholtz's *On the Sensations of Tone,* 1863) to describe intervals. An octave is a 1200 cents. The distance of one half step is 100 cents. Less than 100 is something smaller than a half step. In the West, all intervals are even; the distances between all notes one half step apart are equal and divisible by half steps. The intervals in the Middle Eastern systems are not necessarily even.

WESTERN	WESTERN NOTES	AL-FARABI	ARABIC	AL-URMAWI	TURKISH
0	C	0	C	0	C
50		66	C𝄲		
100	C♯/D♭	90	C♯/D♭		
150		180	D𝄳		
200	D	204	D	204	D
250		270	D𝄲		
300	D♯/E♭	294	D♯/E♭		
350		384	E𝄳		
400	E	408	E	355	E
450		432	E𝄲/F♭		
500	F	498	F	498	F
550		522	F𝄲		
600	F♯/G♭	612	F♯/G♭		
650		636	G𝄳		
700	G	702	G	702	G
750		726	G𝄲		
800	G♯/A♭	792	G♯/A♭		
850		816	A𝄳		
900	A	906	A	853	A
950		930	A𝄲		
1000	A♯/B♭	1020	A♯/B♭		
1050		1044	B𝄳		
1100	B	1086	B	996	B
1150		1134	B𝄲/C♭		
1200	C	1200	C	1200	C

Notice that within the Turkish (al-Urmawi) system there are only seven notes. These are the major scale equivalent tones. From each of the seven notes, there are five different intervals that can be played, thus creating many different ways in which an octave can be divided. Each different makkam (Turkish spelling for maqam) uses a specific group. The five different Turkish intervals are:

Turkish name	English description	Cents
bakiye	small half step	90
kucuk mucennep	large half step	114
buyuk mucennep	small whole step	180
tanini	whole step	204
artik ikili	augmented 2nd	271

The Mashrig, the Mahgrib and the Arabian peninsula (see page 5) all use the same system of dividing an octave, however the modal systems that are extracted from the 24 or 25 possible notes differ from region to region. The Arabs call there modal system *Rast*, the Persians call their system of 12 modes *Dhagsta*.

THE PERSIAN DHAGSTA SYSTEM

Much like the maqam system of Rast, Persian classical music is all based on the *Radif*, which is the repertory of art music comprised of over 300 "tunes" known as *gusheha*, (plural of *gusheh*), based on the 12 modes of the Dhastgah. The *Dhastgaha* (plural of Dhastgah) are the Persian equivilent of the Arabic or Turkish maqam/makkam. The 12 modes of the Dhastgah are divided into two groups, seven basic and five derivative. Here they are, built on C. Like the Rast system, there are half flats and half sharps used to create the modes. The tanbur has movable frets in order to accomadate the "in-between notes," the tar has 25 frets, each a quarter step apart. Those modes that are still known and used today are shown starting on C.

12 DHASTGAH

Basic

1. *mahur* C D E F G A B C
2. *shur* C D𝄳 E♭ F G A♭ B♭
3. *homayun* C D E F G A♭ B♭
4. *segah* C D𝄳 E𝄳 F G𝄳 A𝄳 B𝄳 C
5. *tchahargah* C D𝄳 E F G A𝄳 B C
6. *rastpanjgah*
7. *nava*

Derivative

1. *afshari* C D E𝄳 F G A𝄳 B♭ C
2. *bayat e tork* C D E F G A B𝄳 C
3. *esfahan*
4. *abu-ata*
5. *dashti*